P9-CBT-990

. . . a resource of student activities
to accompany *Write Source*

WRITE SOURCE®

GREAT SOURCE EDUCATION GROUP
a Houghton Mifflin Company
Wilmington, Massachusetts

A Few Words About the *Write Source SkillsBook:*

Before you begin . . .

The *SkillsBook* provides you with opportunities to practice editing and proofreading skills presented in *Write Source*. That book contains guidelines, examples, and models to help you complete your work in the *SkillsBook*.

Each *SkillsBook* activity includes a brief introduction to the topic and examples showing how to complete that activity. You will be directed to the page numbers in *Write Source* for additional information and examples. The "Proofreading Activities" focus on punctuation and the mechanics of writing. The "Sentence Activities" provide practice in sentence combining and in correcting common sentence problems. The "Language Activities" highlight each of the eight parts of speech.

Most activities include The Next Step at the end of the exercise. The purpose of The Next Step is to provide ideas for follow-up work that will help you apply what you have learned to your own writing.

Authors: Pat Sebranek and Dave Kemper

Credits: *Hemera:* pages 75 and 125

Trademarks and trade names are shown in this book strictly for illustrative purposes and are the property of their respective owners. The authors' references herein should not be regarded as affecting their validity.

Copyright © 2006 by Great Source Education Group, a division of Houghton Mifflin Company.
All rights reserved.

Permission is hereby granted to teachers who have purchased the **Write Source Teacher's Resource Package**, grade 5 (ISBN 978-0-669-51842-9 or 0-669-51842-5), to photocopy in classroom quantities, for use by one teacher and his or her students only, the pages in this work that carry a copyright notice, provided each copy made shows the copyright notice. Such copies may not be sold, and further distribution is expressly prohibited. Teachers who have purchased only the *Write Source SkillsBook* (ISBN 978-0-669-51820-7 or 0-669-51820-4) may not reproduce or transmit this work or portions thereof in any other form or by any other electronic or mechanical means, including any information storage or retrieval system, unless expressly permitted by federal copyright law or authorized in writing by Great Source Education Group. Address inquiries to Permissions, Great Source Education Group, 181 Ballardvale Street, Wilmington, MA 01887.

Great Source and **Write Source** are registered trademarks of Houghton Mifflin Company.

Printed in the United States of America

International Standard Book Number: 978-0-669-51820-7 (student edition)
International Standard Book Number: 0-669-51820-4 (student edition)

4 5 6 7 8 9 10 -POO- 10 09 08 07

International Standard Book Number: 978-0-669-51825-2 (teacher's edition)
International Standard Book Number: 0-669-51825-5 (teacher's edition)

4 5 6 7 8 9 10 -POO- 10 09 08 07

Table of Contents

Proofreading Activities

Marking Punctuation

End Punctuation 1 and 2 **3**
Commas Between Items in a Series **5**
Commas in Compound Sentences **7**
Commas to Separate Introductory Phrases and Clauses **9**
Commas in Dates and Addresses **11**
Commas to Set Off Interruptions and Interjections **13**
Commas to Separate Equal Adjectives **15**
Commas to Set Off Appositives **16**
Commas to Set Off Explanatory Phrases **17**
Comma Review 1 and 2 **18**
Commas and End Punctuation Review **20**
Apostrophes 1, 2, 3, and Review **21**
Quotation Marks 1 and 2 **25**
Punctuating Dialogue and Review **27**
Hyphens **29**
Colons 1 and 2 **31**
Semicolons **35**
Italics and Underlining **36**
Italics and Quotation Marks **37**
Dashes **39**
Parentheses **40**
Punctuation Review 1 and 2 **41**

Editing for Mechanics

Capitalization 1 and 2 **45**
Plurals 1 and 2 **49**
Abbreviations **51**
Numbers 1 and 2 **53**

Improving Spelling

Becoming a Better Speller **55**
Proofreading Practice **56**
Spelling Rules 1, 2, 3, 4, and Review 1 and 2 **57**

Using the Right Word

Using the Right Word 1-10 and Review **63**

Sentence Activities

Sentence Basics

Simple Subjects and Predicates 77
Compound Subjects and Predicates 79
Clauses 81
Prepositional Phrases 83

Sentence Problems

Fragments 1 and 2 85
Run-On Sentences 1 and 2 89
Rambling Sentences 1 and 2 91
Double Negatives 93
Sentence Errors Review 1 and 2 94
Subject-Verb Agreement 1, 2, and 3 97
Subject-Verb Agreement Review 1 and 2 101

Sentence Variety

Combining Sentences Using Key Words 103
Combining Sentences with a Series of Words or Phrases 1 and 2 105
Combining Sentences with Phrases 109
Combining Sentences with Compound Subjects and Predicates 111
Kinds of Sentences 1 and 2 113
Types of Sentences 1 and 2 115
Simple and Compound Sentences 117
Compound Sentences 118
Complex Sentences 1 and 2 119
Expanding Sentences with Prepositional Phrases 122
Sentence Variety Review 1 and 2 123

Language Activities

Nouns

Nouns 127
Common and Proper Nouns 129
Concrete and Abstract Nouns 131
Singular and Plural Nouns 133
Gender of Nouns 134
Uses of Nouns 135
Nouns as Objects 137

Pronouns

Person of a Pronoun 139
Number of Pronouns 140
Subject and Object Pronouns 141
Possessive Pronouns 143
Indefinite Pronouns 145
Relative and Demonstrative Pronouns 146
Pronoun-Antecedent Agreement 1 and 2 147

Verbs

Types of Verbs 151
Linking Verbs 152
Helping Verbs 153
Simple Verb Tenses 155
Perfect Tenses 1 and 2 157
Active and Passive Verbs 159
Irregular Verbs 1 and 2 160
Irregular-Verbs Review 162

Adjectives

Proper and Common Adjectives 163
Predicate Adjectives 165
Indefinite Adjectives 166
Forms of Adjectives 167

Adverbs

Types of Adverbs 169
Forms of Adverbs 171

Prepositions

Prepositional Phrases 1 and 2 **173**

Conjunctions

Coordinating Conjunctions **177**
Subordinating Conjunctions **179**
Conjunctions Review **181**

Interjections

Interjections **183**

Parts of Speech

Parts of Speech Review 1, 2, and 3 **184**

Proofreading Activities

Every activity in this section includes sentences that need to be checked for punctuation, mechanics, or usage. Most of the activities also include helpful *Write Source* references. In addition, **The Next Step,** which is at the end of most activities, encourages follow-up practice of certain skills.

Marking Punctuation 3

Editing for Mechanics 45

Improving Spelling 55

Using the Right Word 63

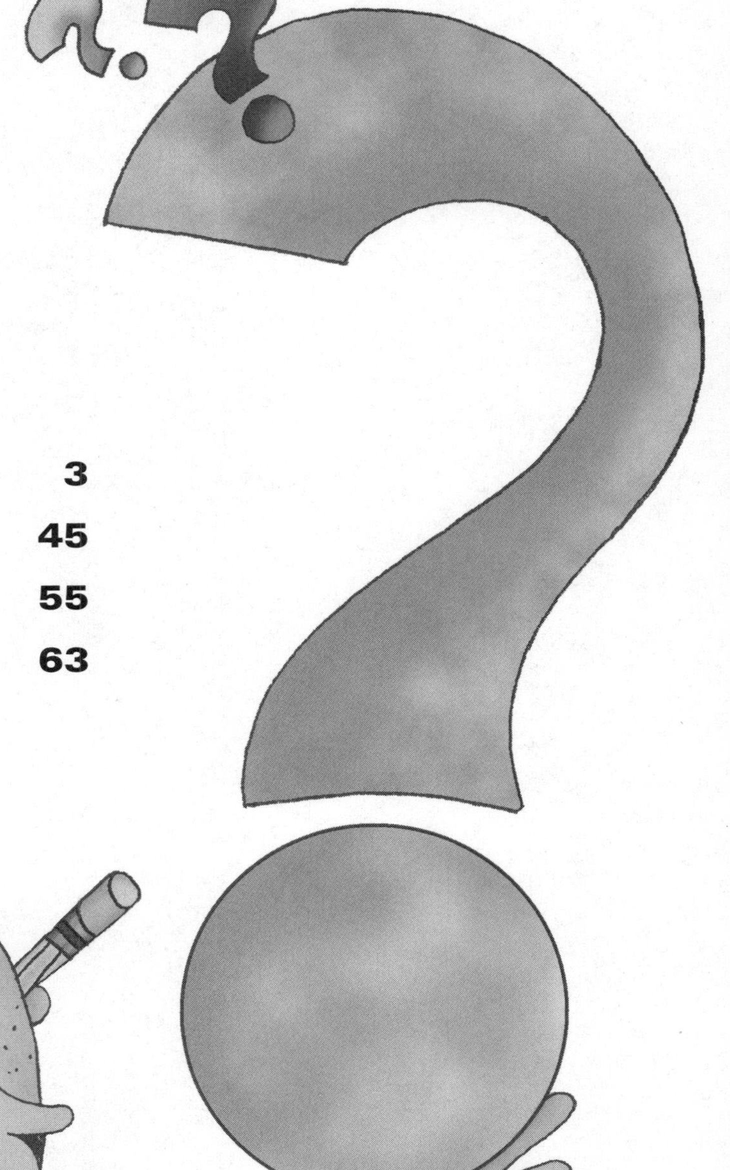

End Punctuation 1

Using the correct **end punctuation** is a basic step in punctuating your writing. There are three kinds of end punctuation: the period, the question mark, and the exclamation point. (See *Write Source* pages 479–480.)

Examples

Native Americans welcomed the Pilgrims.

When was that?

That was back in 1620!

Put the correct end punctuation—a period, a question mark, or an exclamation point—in the sentences below. Capitalize the first letter of each sentence. The first sentence has been done for you.

have you ever wondered who the very first Americans were scientists say they came from Asia thousands of years ago at that time, land connected Asia to the part of North America that is now Alaska imagine that people followed herds of animals across the "land bridge" between Asia and America these people needed to use the animals for food and clothing it was much too cold to grow crops

the first Americans slowly moved farther and farther south after thousands of years, their ancestors reached the tip of South America wow that's a lot of walking

The Next Step **Write a paragraph describing your coldest experience. In at least two places, try to use a word, a phrase, or a sentence that would require an exclamation point.**

© Great Source. All rights reserved. (5)

End Punctuation 2

This activity gives you practice using correct **end punctuation**. (Check pages 479 and 480 in *Write Source* if you need help with this activity.)

Examples

He wears a cape and a big *S*.

Who is he?

He's Superman!

Directions **Put the correct end punctuation in the sentences below, and capitalize the first letter of each sentence. The first sentence has been done for you.**

the first superhero, Superman, came on the scene in the 1930s he was created by a writer and an artist, and their cartoon Superman was no average Joe how fast was Superman he was faster than a speeding bullet he could also bend steel with his bare hands he had these special abilities because he came from a planet called Krypton of course, he always used his powers to fight evil

Superman was in comic books and newspapers and on radio and TV when World War II started, Superman's creators had to decide if he would join the army well, he tried to join the army but failed his eye exam how did he do that with his X-ray vision he read an eye chart in the next room, instead of reading his own

The Next Step **Write a story describing a problem Superman faces. Use the three kinds of end punctuation in your story.**

© Great Source. All rights reserved. (5)

Commas Between Items in a Series

Commas are used between words, phrases, or clauses in a series. (See *Write Source* 482.1.)

Examples

In a Series of Words:
Sprinters tend to be **fit**, **fast**, and **strong**.

In a Series of Phrases:
Runners may win **blue ribbons**, **fancy medals**, or **big trophies**.

In a Series of Clauses:
Sprinters run short distances, **marathoners run long distances**, and **relay runners run as part of a team**.

In the paragraph below, add commas between items in a series. The first sentence has been done for you.

Jesse Owens, an African American track star, was born in Alabama, attended college in Ohio, and won four gold medals in Germany's 1936 Olympics. Owens faced prejudice disappointment and unkindness in the United States. In Germany, he won the 100-meter race the 200-meter race the 400-meter relay race and the broad jump. However, instead of Owens, a white man who had won only one Olympic medal was named best American athlete that year. Many people admired respected and cheered Owens. At a parade for him in New York City, someone threw him a bag containing $10,000.

© Great Source. All rights reserved. (5)

In the following sentences, add commas between items in a series. The first sentence has been done for you.

1. All Olympic runners practice every day, drink lots of fluids, and carefully pace themselves.
2. Some famous women runners are Mary Decker Marion Jones and Florence Joyner.
3. These runners have won titles in national world and Olympic races.
4. All of these women have worked hard overcome injuries and won titles.
5. One was a champion in sprinting one was a winner in middle distance and one was a long-distance title holder.
6. Have you heard about Joan Benoit Samuelson who had a dream pushed toward it and never gave up?
7. She ran in high school in college and in the 1979 Boston Marathon.
8. Joan was an unknown a clear winner and a record breaker.
9. She also won the 1983 Boston Marathon the 1984 U.S. Olympic time trials and the 1984 Olympic Marathon.
10. Three miles into the Olympic race, Benoit Samuelson moved ahead kept the lead and won easily.
11. Joan Benoit Samuelson is a role model an author and an Olympic gold medal winner.

© Great Source. All rights reserved. (5)

Commas in Compound Sentences

A **comma** may be used with a coordinating conjunction to join two independent clauses. Coordinating conjunctions are words such as *and, but,* or *so.* (See *Write Source* 482.3.)

Example

Comma and Coordinating Conjunction:
I know the words to "The Star-Spangled Banner," **but** I can't hit all the notes!

(Note: The comma is placed inside the quotation marks.)

In the paragraph below, add commas between independent clauses joined by coordinating conjunctions. The first sentence has been done for you.

Americans have been singing "The Star-Spangled Banner" since the early 1800s, but it didn't become the official national anthem until 1931. On November 3, 1929, newspapers announced that there was no official anthem so people began to think about a national song. More than 5 million people wrote to ask Congress to choose one but many of these people didn't want "The Star-Spangled Banner." Some people were bothered by two things: the music was written in England and the United States had fought against England for freedom in 1776. "America" and a few other songs received votes but "The Star-Spangled Banner" won the day.

© Great Source. All rights reserved. (5)

Directions **Add a comma and a coordinating conjunction in each blank to complete the following paragraph. The first sentence has been done for you.**

Everyone knows that the national symbol of the United States is the bald eagle, but not many know how Ben Franklin felt about the bird. He wanted the wild turkey to be the symbol. The wild turkey was a proud bird with courage ________ Franklin liked that. Other people thought the strong bald eagle would look better on coins and flags. However, Franklin disliked the eagle ________ he tried to tell everyone about the wild turkey. He even wrote a letter to his daughter about the two birds ________ we still have that letter to read today. Everyone wanted to have a national symbol that belonged to this country. People often saw eagles and turkeys. The bald eagles were seen flying near rivers ________ the turkeys were spotted on the edge of forests. Ben Franklin convinced a lot of people to vote for the wild turkey ________ the eagle was chosen. The bald eagle won with only one more vote than the wild turkey.

The Next Step **Write a short paragraph about something you feel is a good symbol of this country. Try to use several compound sentences in your paragraph.**

© Great Source. All rights reserved. (5)

Commas to Separate Introductory Phrases and Clauses

Commas signal readers to pause after a long phrase or clause that introduces the rest of the sentence. (See *Write Source* 484.1 for more information.)

Examples

After an Introductory Phrase:
At the end of the 1500s, the first pockets were added to clothing.

After an Introductory Clause:
Long before electricity was discovered, a Greek inventor made a clock that was powered by moving water.

In the following sentences, place a comma after the introductory phrase or clause. The first one has been done for you.

1. Ten years after Thomas Adams began producing chewing gum in 1871, bubble gum was developed.

2. Best known as an astronomer Galileo also was an inventor—he invented the thermometer.

3. About 7,500 years ago in Turkey people used a natural glass called *obsidian* for mirrors.

4. A year before Thomas Edison introduced his lightbulb a British inventor made one.

© Great Source. All rights reserved. (5)

5. When one of the first movies was shown people fainted because they thought the train in the movie would run over them!

6. Although we don't think of it as a discovery paper was an invention.

7. Invented in China in 105 C.E. paper now has thousands of uses.

Place a comma after the introductory phrase or clause in each of the following sentences. Then label it as a "phrase" or "clause" on the line in front of the number. The first one has been done for you.

Phrase 1. After much study, Joseph Begun invented the first broadcast tape recorder in 1936.

______ 2. Noticing how burrs stuck to his socks George de Mestral created the Velcro fastener.

______ 3. After Edwin Budding and John Ferrabee of England grew tired of cutting grass by hand they invented the lawn mover.

______ 4. During World War II Percy Spencer discovered that microwaves could cook food.

______ 5. Because he was worried about his patients' survival Joseph Lister introduced antiseptic surgery in 1867.

The Next Step Write three sentences of your own that use introductory phrases or clauses. Share your sentences with a classmate. Who used the longest introductory phrase or clause?

© Great Source. All rights reserved. (5)

Commas in Dates and Addresses

Commas are used to separate items in dates and addresses. (See *Write Source* 484.2.)

Examples

To Separate Items in Dates:
The first drive-in opened on **June 6, 1933**.

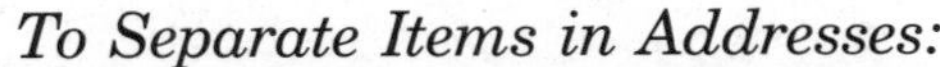

To Separate Items in Addresses:
The address of the president and the first lady is **1600 Pennsylvania Avenue NW, Washington, D.C. 20050**.

In the sentences below, add commas to separate items in dates and addresses. The first one has been done for you.

1. On January 21, 1954, the United States launched the first atomic-powered submarine, *Nautilus.*
2. United States president William H. Harrison died on April 4 1841 just one month after his inauguration.
3. John H. Glenn, Jr., became the first American to orbit the earth on February 20 1962.
4. The Central Pacific and Union Pacific Railroads met in Promontory, Utah, on May 10 1869 to form a transcontinental railroad.
5. My birth date is April 23 1992.
6. On September 9 1850 California became the 31st state.

© Great Source. All rights reserved. (5)

7. On October 27 1920 KOKA in Philadelphia, Pennsylvania, became the first licensed radio station in the United States.

8. The Brazilian team made soccer history on July 22 1994 when they defeated Italy and won the World Cup for the fourth time.

9. The official address of the British Prime Minister has always been 10 Downing Street London England.

10. On November 3 1998 voters in Minnesota elected former professional wrestler Jesse "The Body" Ventura as governor.

11. The new health center is located at 33412 Strasser Court Belton City Arkansas.

12. Senator John Glenn boarded the space shuttle *Discovery* on October 29 1998 for his first return to space since 1962.

13. For many years, the control center for space flights has been in Houston Texas.

14. What will you be doing on June 10 2025?

15. I want the candy sent to 3034 West Ring Drive Bellagreen Arkansas.

The Next Step **Write a news story announcing the unveiling of a new car. Use dates to tell when each of the car's special new features was first developed. Use addresses to explain where the parts were made or assembled. Use commas correctly!**

© Great Source. All rights reserved. (5)

Commas to Set Off Interruptions and Interjections

Commas are used to set off a word, phrase, or clause that interrupts the main thought of the sentence. Commas are also used to separate an interjection from the rest of the sentence. (See *Write Source* 486.1 and 486.2.)

Examples

Interruption: This book, **as a matter of fact**, belongs to Francesca.

Interjections: **Wow**, I didn't know that.

In the following sentences, correctly set off the interruptions or interjections with commas. (*Note:* One of the sentences does not need a comma.)

1. Did you know for example that butterflies are insects?
2. No kidding I thought they were small birds like hummingbirds.
3. There are in fact butterflies that grow as big as some birds.
4. Hmm are you sure?
5. Yes I read about it in this book.
6. Wow listen to this! Butterflies have tiny scales on their wings.
7. The scales are so tiny however that the wings look painted.
8. Well I thought only fish had scales.
9. Butterflies believe it or not do have scales.
10. Wait a minute I thought you said butterflies are insects.

© Great Source. All rights reserved. (5)

11. All insects have six legs don't they?

12. Hey that's right!

13. Look here the butterflies on page 244 have only four legs.

14. You are right hmm.

15. Wait there are front legs held against the butterfly's body.

16. Oh now I see the tiny front legs.

The Next Step **Write a paragraph about fish, birds, or snakes. Use some interjections and interruptions in several of the sentences. Be sure you properly set off the interjections and interruptions with commas.**

© Great Source. All rights reserved. (5)

Commas to Separate Equal Adjectives

If two or more adjectives equally modify a noun, separate them with a **comma**. How can you tell if the adjectives are equal? Reverse the order of the adjectives. If the meaning of the sentence does not change, the adjectives are equal.

Examples

Two Adjectives That Modify a Noun Equally:
Jen thought the **cool, clear** water tasted good.
(Jen thought the **clear, cool** water tasted good.)

Two Adjectives That Do Not Modify the Noun Equally:
Evans picked up the **silver wedding** ring.
(Evans picked up the **wedding silver** ring.)

In the following paragraph, put commas between equal adjectives. The first one has been done for you. (See *Write Source* 488.1 for more information.)

Because Rafer liked doing tricks, he needed a strong, sturdy scooter. He really liked the new popular Laser J55 model, but it cost almost $60. One day he saw an ad on the school bulletin board for a four-year-old Jet B37 scooter for $10. This would be a cheap dependable scooter until he could get a Laser. The scooter had faded streaked paint on the deck. He could tell the deck had a thin sharp edge on one side, but his dad could fix that. Rafer liked the looks of the chrome wheelie bar, but he didn't like the thick hard wheels. After he used the scooter, he decided he really liked it.

© Great Source. All rights reserved. (5)

Commas to Set Off Appositives

Commas are used in many different ways. Commas set off **appositives**. An appositive is a word or phrase that *renames* or *explains* a noun that comes before the word or phrase. (See *Write Source* 488.2.)

Example

Cooper Elementary, **my school**, has 250 students.

Use commas to set off the appositives in the following paragraph. The first sentence has been done for you.

Mrs. Chang, our teacher, won an award. The award a gift certificate was for being an excellent teacher. Our principal Mrs. Greene presented the award. Mrs. Chang the best teacher I've had yet deserved to win. Alisha a girl in our class read a poem about Mrs. Chang. Mrs. Chang's husband a math teacher was there. The rest of us sang a song "You're the Best" for Mrs. Chang. Bobby a talented composer wrote the song. We all wrote stories favorite classroom memories to put in a booklet for our great teacher. Tamara a computer whiz made a banner on her computer. The banner a work of art said, "Way to go, Mrs. Chang!"

The Next Step **Write four sentences, each one saying something about a different person you know. Start each sentence with the person's name, add an appositive that tells something about the person, and then finish the sentence.**

© Great Source. All rights reserved. (5)

Commas to Set Off Explanatory Phrases

Commas are used to set off **explanatory phrases** from the rest of the sentence. Explanatory phrases add information. (See *Write Source* 488.2.)

Example

SpaceShipOne, **funded by a private company**, set an altitude record.

Directions **Use commas to set off the explanatory phrases in the following sentences.**

1. Mike Melvill the first commercial astronaut to pilot *SpaceShipOne* flew the craft at more than 1,800 miles per hour.
2. A jet called the *White Knight* built by a company called Scaled Composites carried the spacecraft to 50,000 feet.
3. On October 4, 2004, Brian Binnie the second pilot to fly *SpaceShipOne* felt the powerful rocket climb into space.
4. Then the rocket its engines shut off reached a record 69.6 miles.
5. Melvill's and Binnie's flights completed within a week of each other meant Scaled Composites won a $10 million prize.
6. A special group made up of people wanting to promote space travel first offered the Ansari X Prize back in May 1996.
7. Richard Branson hoping to take paying travelers into space announced his new company would charge $200,000 per ride.

© Great Source. All rights reserved. (5)

Comma Review 1

This activity is a review of the different ways in which you've learned to use commas. (Review *Write Source* pages 482–488.)

Directions ▶ **Add commas where they are needed in the following paragraph.**

If you sometimes feel like sleeping all winter you might in fact like to have a groundhog's life. Groundhogs also known as woodchucks sleep for six months every year. Wow that's a long winter's nap. Although Groundhog Day is February 2 groundhogs rarely wake up before April! While a groundhog hibernates its body temperature drops, and its heart rate slows down. Bears raccoons and skunks which at least wake up for midwinter snacks don't sleep as deeply as groundhogs. Insects reptiles and amphibians also hibernate but they don't sleep as deeply as groundhogs either. Insects hide under tree bark beneath logs and in leaf litter. Amphibians which can easily dry out burrow into mud to escape the cold. While turtles often dig into the mud as well snakes find caves old wells or wood piles for the long winter. In fact groundhogs some of the deepest sleeping of all hibernating creatures are rarely seen in winter and now you know why.

© Great Source. All rights reserved. (5)

Comma Review 2

This activity is a review of the different ways in which you've learned to use commas. (Review *Write Source* pages 482–488.)

Add commas to correctly punctuate the following sentences.

1. On July 20 1969 Neil Armstrong was the first person to walk on the moon.
2. Sally Ride an astronaut flew into space in 1983.
3. Lewis and Clark's famous historic journey began on May 14 1804 and ended on September 23 1806.
4. The Apollo program planned for moon exploration began in 1963.
5. Lincoln delivered his Gettysburg Address on November 19 1863.
6. In the Civil War General Robert E. Lee surrendered on April 9 1865 and the last Southern soldiers surrendered on May 26 1865.
7. Parking for Independence Hall is at 1518 Walnut Street Philadelphia Pennsylvania.
8. The largest most-powerful rocket ever built was the *Saturn V.*
9. Hawaii became the 50th state on August 21 1959.
10. The White House is located at 1600 West Pennsylvania Avenue N.W. Washington D.C.

© Great Source. All rights reserved. (5)

Commas and End Punctuation Review

This activity is a review of commas and end punctuation. (See *Write Source* pages 479–488.)

Add needed commas and end punctuation marks in the sentences below. Also capitalize the first letter of each new sentence. The first sentence has been done for you.

in the early 1800s only about half of the children in the United States went to school at that time, many people thought that only boys should go to school so girls were usually not allowed to attend

However, Sara Pierce started a school for girls and she taught the girls grammar reading writing and history one of her students was Harriet Beecher Stowe ms. Stowe later wrote a famous novel called *Uncle Tom's Cabin* Mary Lyon founded the first college to accept women and that college was called Mount Holyoke College Emily Dickinson another great writer was a student there

one teacher became famous for writing books for both boys and girls he wrote the first American dictionary and his name is still on many dictionaries can you guess his name sure you can his name is Noah Webster

© Great Source. All rights reserved. (5)

Apostrophes 1

Apostrophes are sometimes used to make contractions. (See *Write Source* 490.1.)

Examples

you + will = **you'll** I + am = **I'm**

have + not = **haven't** would + not = **wouldn't**

In the following paragraph, use apostrophes to make as many contractions as you can. The first one has been done for you.

Jessica ~~does not~~ *doesn't* like to sit in class on warm spring days. She would rather be out playing baseball with Juan and Jennifer. They are all baseball nuts. They will spend all summer playing baseball, I am sure. Jessica always says it is too nice to be inside, even if it is raining. I like baseball, too, but I do not like to play in the rain. On rainy days, I would rather play computer games, but that does not last. Those games can not hold my attention for long. The sound of the rain on the window makes me want to sleep. I know I should not take a nap in the afternoon, but I can not keep my eyes open. Suddenly, I will awaken and discover it is supper time. That means I will not be able to go to my best friend's house. I will have to stay up late to finish my homework. Maybe I should not play computer games on a rainy day.

The Next Step **Write a sentence for each of the following word groups using the contraction form: *I am*, *you are*, *could not*, *it will*, and *they would*.**

© Great Source. All rights reserved. (5)

Apostrophes 2

Apostrophes are sometimes used to show possession. (See 490.2 and 492.1.)

Examples

Singular Possession: The **nurse's** stethoscope was missing.

Plural Possession: The **nurses'** station had three nurses.

In this paragraph, add apostrophes where they are needed to form singular and plural possessives. The first one has been done for you.

Peoples dreams of future careers often involve helping those in need. From the age of 11, Clara Bartons goal was to be a nurse. A brothers illness showed her that she liked to help sick people. Later, with her fathers permission, she went to help soldiers in the Civil War. Clara found out there weren't enough bandages for soldiers wounds. She decided to do something. With some senators support, Clara was able to bring much needed medical supplies to the battlefield. Often she stood by doctors sides as bullets whizzed by. Several years after the war, she traveled to Europe to help the wounded and suffering during the Franco-Prussian War. Because she was so impressed with the International Red Crosss work, she later founded Americas Red Cross in 1881. Clara traveled many times to help several countries starving people. Clara Barton will always be remembered for her unselfish devotion to the worlds people.

© Great Source. All rights reserved. (5)

Apostrophes 3

Apostrophes are sometimes used to show some plurals and shared possession. (To get ready, review *Write Source* 492.3–492.4.)

Examples

To Form Some Plurals:
It is an invention with **+ 's** and **– 's**.

To Show Shared Possession:
Tom and **Marci's** calculator is powered by sunlight.

Directions **Add apostrophes where they are needed in the following sentences.**

1. Young students need to learn their A, B, Cs.
2. Fern, Bill, and Jacks science project is due this week.
3. How many 5828s are there in the national phone system?
4. That paragraph has too many "becauses" in it.
5. I was told to pick up John and Michelles homework.
6. Why are there so many +s in this math problem?
7. This award is Jane, Tony, Saul, and Jakes.
8. Antoine's report card had two As, four Bs, and no Cs.
9. The boys and girls playground has new equipment.
10. As Phil checked his story, he saw he had too many "awesomes" in it.

© Great Source. All rights reserved. (5)

Apostrophes Review

Directions **Add all the apostrophes needed in the following sentences. Form plurals, contractions, and possessive nouns using apostrophes.**

1. An oil tankers anchor weighs hundreds of pounds.
2. Big ships can not stop quickly.
3. Arlene, Rafe, and Sues cruise ship leaves for the Caribbean tomorrow.
4. Boys clothes are in aisle 15 next to boots and shoes.
5. Football coaches like to use Xs and Os when drawing plays on the blackboard.
6. I think you will like the color of your new bike.
7. Do not forget to bring your notebooks to class on Thursday.
8. Jared likes to draw 9s and 15s all over the cover of his notebook.
9. Sharks, bears, and wolves jaws are very strong.
10. Tom said he would rather paint a fence than do nothing all day.
11. He knew his paper needed reworking when he saw all the !s and *s.
12. Place the girls team jerseys on the table.

© Great Source. All rights reserved. (5)

Quotation Marks 1

What do **quotation marks** mark? They mark the exact words a person speaks. They are also used to mark the titles of songs, poems, short stories, articles, and so on. (See *Write Source* page 494.)

Example

"Hi," Angelo said. "Where are you going?"

Add quotation marks where they are needed in the following sentences. The first sentence has been done for you.

1. Ricardo said, "I'm going to the library. Do you want to come?"
2. No, I answered. But will you check out a book for me?
3. Sure, Ricardo said. What book do you want?
4. I asked for any book that included nature poems like the poem Birdfoot's Grampa or the poem Something Told the Wild Geese.
5. Here are some great poems by Joseph Bruchac, Ricardo said.
6. I told him I hadn't read any of Joseph Bruchac's poems yet, but I saw one called The Song of Small Things in my literature book.
7. Be sure to read it, Ric said. It's awesome!
8. I will, I said. If all the poems are about nature, I'll like them!

The Next Step **Write down a conversation you and a friend have had about school, sports, books, or movies. Be sure to use quotation marks correctly.**

© Great Source. All rights reserved. (5)

Quotation Marks 2

Quotation marks are used to set off dialogue. (See the "Sample Dialogue" in *Write Source* on page 109 and also see page 494.)

Example "Soccer is my favorite sport," Maria said.

Rewrite the dialogue below about a soccer game. Add quotation marks where they are needed. Also start a new paragraph each time a different person speaks.

Did you see the game yesterday? Rodrigo shouted as he jogged up the steps leading to the art room. Yeah, it was great! Maria shouted back. I didn't think we had a chance. I mean, two goals to zero with only two minutes—I know! Rodrigo interrupted. I switched the channel twice before I realized what was happening. What a rally! Now it's the semifinals against Brazil, whispered Maria as they headed for their seats in the front row.

© Great Source. All rights reserved. (5)

Punctuating Dialogue

Written dialogue follows definite rules for using quotation marks, commas, end marks, and capital letters. (See *Write Source* pages 116–117 and 494.)

Example

"Hey, Craig!" yelled Bill. "Wait for me!"

Write in any missing punctuation in the following dialogue. Also correct any errors in capitalization.

Hi, Bill I said. Did you buy any new baseball cards at the store

Yes, I did Bill answered with a smile. I had enough money to buy 10 packs.

Great did you open the packs yet

No do you want to help me?

Sure! I hope you get some doubles I said. I will buy them from you.

Maybe we could trade Bill answered.

Let's open the packs and see what you got first

Okay, and you think about which of your cards you'd like to trade

© Great Source. All rights reserved. (5)

Punctuating Dialogue Review

Directions **In the following dialogue sentences, add the correct end punctuation, quotation marks, and capitalization.**

Wait a minute Jorge said Sonja wants you to take her article to the newspaper

Sanchez said what article

Jorge answered it's her article about our field trip last week to the mint

Oh, that one said Sanchez am I in the story

Yes, you are

I want to see what she wrote! exclaimed Sanchez It was fun.

Sonja wrote about all of us and the trip, but she singles you out for praise responded Jorge.

Why did she do that Sanchez asked

you helped Terry get around in his wheelchair, Jorge said.

I didn't mind doing that, said Sanchez. My sister has to use crutches, so I am used to helping.

Well, whether you are used to it or not, replied Jorge, Sonja was impressed with your kindness.

© Great Source. All rights reserved. (5)

Hyphens

Hyphens are explained on *Write Source* page 496. The following activities give you practice using hyphens.

Examples

With Compound Adjectives:
My sister chews **sugar-free** gum.

Between Syllables:
She also likes to eat frozen orange juice **con-centrate** right from the can.

With Compound Words:
The **president-elect** waits more than two months to take office.

Put hyphens where they are needed in the sentences below. The first sentence has been done for you.

1. Mom puts big pieces of chocolate in her chocolate-chunk cookies.
2. The governor elect has a lot to learn about her new job.
3. My great grandfather was a well known doctor.
4. I once made a long distance call to Japan.
5. I have an eight year old cousin who looks like me.
6. Dad's sister in law took a well deserved vacation.
7. Jon is an all purpose running back for our team.
8. My friend Sam likes well done hamburgers.
9. They covered the roof with blue green tiles.

© Great Source. All rights reserved. (5)

Directions Use hyphens to show how you could divide the following words at the end of a line. (Some words should not be divided.)

1. history ___his-to-ry___
2. writing __________
3. item __________
4. revise __________
5. improving __________
6. contents __________
7. connection __________
8. microscope __________
9. anyone __________
10. doesn't __________

Directions Using the compound words listed below, fill in the blanks to complete the story.

well-timed fun-filled well-known old-fashioned
well-equipped far-distant sun-warmed

Most of the class had never seen a lake as big as Lake Erie. Some thought the __________ lake looked like the ocean. Because Lake Erie is so wide, the students could not see the __________ shore. Before going on their __________ trip, they found out that four states and one province border Lake Erie. The students also learned that __________ boats catch more fish in Erie than the other four Great Lakes combined. The reason is that the __________ lake is so shallow that fish seem to do well. The class had fun learning about Lake Erie, seeing the lake, and riding on an __________ tour boat. Still, everyone agreed that a __________ swim was a good way to end the day.

© Great Source. All rights reserved. (5)

Colons 1

A **colon** can be used to introduce a list in a sentence and to express time. (See *Write Source* page 498.)

Examples

I am interested in the following mammals: whales, dolphins, and porpoises.

Our field trip departed for the zoo at 8:30 a.m. on Tuesday.

Add colons to introduce the lists in the sentences below. Also add colons to express time. The first sentence has been done for you.

1. Reptiles have the following things in common: they have backbones, most hatch their young from eggs, and they are cold-blooded.
2. The following are all reptiles turtles, alligators, and crocodiles.
3. Alligators and crocodiles have some things in common they have webbed feet, their eyes and nostrils are high on their heads, and they are able to open their mouths underwater without drowning.
4. There are two ways to identify alligators by their rounded snouts and by their upper teeth, which are seen even when their mouths are closed!
5. Here are the telltale signs of a crocodile a pointed snout and two lower teeth sticking out when its mouth is closed.

© Great Source. All rights reserved. (5)

6. The following are all amphibians salamanders, frogs, and toads.

7. In the Everglades, you can see alligators at the Gulf Coast Visitor Center from 900 a.m. to 430 p.m. all summer.

8. Outside the park, airboat tours run from 800 a.m. to 500 p.m.

Directions **In the paragraph below, add colons to introduce the lists and to express time.**

Florida is home to three interesting lizards geckos, glass lizards, and iguanids. Lizards are very similar to snakes; however, unlike snakes, most lizards have three features legs, external ear openings, and eyelids. Geckos are most active in the early evening from 500 to 700. They can do two interesting things they can quickly shed their tails (which regenerate), and they can walk upside down across ceilings. Glass lizards are known as “glass snakes” for two reasons their long tails break off very easily, and they have no legs. These lizards enjoy certain “bugs” for dinner crickets, grasshoppers, and spiders. Iguanids are the lizards often called “chameleons.” Besides changing color to blend with their surroundings, these lizards seem to enjoy three activities head bobbing, head nodding, and push-ups.

The Next Step **Write a sentence of your own about a favorite animal. Include a colon to introduce a list.**

© Great Source. All rights reserved. (5)

Colons 2

Another way a **colon** is used is to make a formal introduction of a quotation. (See *Write Source* 498.2.)

Example

Joan Lowery Nixon said this about writing: "The idea is just the beginning of the story."

Directions **Add colons where they are needed in the following sentences.**

1. On the subject of honesty, Mark Twain said this "Truth is stranger than fiction—to some people."
2. I thought of something Abraham Lincoln said "It's a good rule never to send a mouse to catch a skunk, or a polliwog to tackle a whale."
3. I was scared, and I remembered this line from *The Lion, the Witch, and the Wardrobe* "Peter did not feel very brave; indeed, he felt he was going to be sick."
4. In *The Adventures of Sherlock Holmes*, Holmes says this about life "My dear fellow, life is infinitely stranger than anything the mind of man could invent."

© Great Source. All rights reserved. (5)

5. Ben Franklin wrote in his *Poor Richard's Almanac* "Well done is better than well said."

6. When interviewed about his space flight, Russian cosmonaut Yuri Gagarin excitedly said "I could have gone on flying through space forever."

The Next Step **Now write three sentences of your own in which you use colons to introduce quotations. (Look them up in a book of quotations, or take them from a favorite book.)**

1. ____

____

____

____

2. ____

____

____

____

3. ____

____

____

____

© Great Source. All rights reserved. (5)

Semicolons

Semicolons tell the reader to pause, or even stop, before reading the rest of the sentence. (See *Write Source* page 500.)

Examples

To Join Two Independent Clauses:
I have a cat; he's a blur of gray fur.

To Separate Groups in a Series with Commas:
I need to **buy cat food, cat toys, and litter; clean the cat box, hallway, and closet;** and **give Fuzzball a brushing.**

Each sentence below contains two independent clauses that are separated by a comma and a conjunction. Replace the comma and conjunction with a semicolon. The first sentence has been done for you.

Roy C. Sullivan was a park ranger, yet his life was more exciting than you might think. He was struck by lightning seven times, but he lived to tell about it. No one understood why Sullivan kept getting hit by lightning, and it's amazing that he kept working! Lightning "fired" several of his hats, and one time it set fire to his hair.

The Next Step **Write a sentence using the set of phrases below. Be sure to use semicolons appropriately in your new sentence.**

see the lions, tigers, and bears ■ eat hot dogs, ice cream, and cotton candy ■ run home in time for supper

© Great Source. All rights reserved. (5)

Italics and Underlining

Italics are explained on *Write Source* page 502. In many publications, titles of books are shown in italics. However you may **underline** book, newspaper, magazine, and movie titles in your writing.

Example

Louisa May Alcott wrote Little Women, a book about her family.

Directions **In the following sentences, underline all titles that should be in italics.**

1. Washington Irving wrote a book of stories called The Sketch Book. Rip Van Winkle, who slept for 20 years, is a character in it.
2. Phillis Wheatley was a slave who was brought to America when she was about seven. She never went to school, but she wrote poetry that was published in London Magazine.
3. James Fenimore Cooper wrote about the sea and pioneer life. He wrote successful novels like The Last of the Mohicans, The Prairie, and The Deerslayer.
4. Early American writers created tall tales about larger-than-life heroes. Modern writer Steven Kellogg also wrote tall tales and made two of them into books called Paul Bunyan and Pecos Bill.

© Great Source. All rights reserved. (5)

Italics and Quotation Marks

To punctuate titles in your writing, the general rule is that titles of complete works (such as books) are italicized or underlined. Titles of parts of works (such as chapters) are put in quotation marks.

Write Source 494.3 explains which titles need quotation marks, and 502.1 explains which titles should be italicized or underlined.

Examples

My favorite chapter in <u>Write Source</u> is "Writing Poems."

"Too Many Cats!" is a story in a book called <u>Cat Tales</u>.

In the following sentences, put quotation marks around the titles that need them, and underline titles that should be in italic type.

1. The Lion King and Aladdin are movies with great songs.
2. Our science book has chapters called The Planets and Beyond and Rivers and Seas.
3. Part of a poem called The New Colossus by Emma Lazarus is written on the Statue of Liberty.
4. Little Richard sings Old MacDonald on his kids' album called Shake It All About.
5. Mom likes to watch The Simpsons.
6. My dad reads two newspapers, the Atlanta Constitution and the Wall Street Journal, plus Time magazine.

© Great Source. All rights reserved. (5)

Directions

Write five sentences, each one including one of the following titles: your favorite song, CD, TV show, movie, and book. Punctuate the titles correctly.

1. (song)

2. (CD)

3. (TV show)

4. (movie)

5. (book)

© Great Source. All rights reserved. (5)

Dashes

A **dash** is used to show a break or change in direction in a sentence. (See *Write Source* page 504.)

Example

Sometimes Laura puts grape or cranberry juice—how weird—on her cereal.

Add dashes where they are needed in the following sentences. The first one has been done for you.

1. My brothers read all the Goosebumps books—I love the name *Goosebumps*—by R. L. Stine.
2. Christopher Pike maybe you've heard of him also writes scary books.
3. I must go to the dentist my least favorite thing to do after school.
4. We walked all the way home imagine this wearing our costumes.
5. Gary said and I don't believe it that he finished his homework.
6. Sarah isn't coming I don't know why so don't wait for her.
7. What's that old song Amber was singing it about the bayou?
8. Ben he's so lucky is moving to Florida.

The Next Step **Write four sentences that use dashes correctly. The sentences can tell a story, or each sentence can be about a different topic.**

© Great Source. All rights reserved. (5)

Parentheses

Parentheses are used to separate words or phrases added to a sentence to make it clearer. (See *Write Source* 504.4.)

Example

The high-speed commuter train (The Coast Flyer) runs every day at 6:00 a.m. and 5:00 p.m.

Directions **Read the following sentences and add parentheses where they are needed.**

1. Felicia's father works in Evanston a Chicago suburb.
2. She says that he gets up very early around 4:30 a.m. to catch the train to Evanston.
3. He likes his job working with electricity and living in the suburbs.
4. Sometimes he wires new homes, but often his work is in older homes with outdated wiring.
5. Felicia sometimes worries about dangers bare wires and downed power lines that her father has to handle.
6. She knows that electricity a powerful force can be very dangerous.
7. Her dad tells her he's very careful no daydreaming on the job.
8. Her mother reminds Felicia about his numerous awards for safety.

© Great Source. All rights reserved. (5)

Punctuation Review 1

The following paragraphs use different kinds of punctuation that you have practiced. Use "Marking Punctuation" on *Write Source* pages 479–505 to help you.

In the following paragraphs, most of the punctuation marks are missing. Correct the paragraphs by adding commas, apostrophes, semicolons, hyphens, and end punctuation. The first sentence has been done for you.

The game of Monopoly is popular now, but it didn't start out that way. Charles Darrow, the inventor, tried to sell the game to Parker Brothers Company but they didnt want to buy it Parker Brothers said Darrows game took too long to play, had mistakes in the instructions and wouldnt sell Darrow had a few Monopoly games made and he paid for them himself Monopoly became very popular so Parker Brothers decided to buy it after all Monopoly became the best selling game of all time in fact, more Monopoly money than real money is printed every year How do you think Charles Darrow would have felt about this

One day a businessman in England decided that the game would sell well in that country but he thought local street names were needed Also he decided to have British pounds instead of dollars The Monopoly game is now printed in 26 languages and it

© Great Source. All rights reserved. (5)

is sold in 80 countries Most people who play Monopoly enjoy this slow paced game How can this be Dont people prefer the faster pace of computer games Of course, some do enjoy the speed but millions more like Monopoly

I heard there was a tournament at Peters Township Public Library 616 E. McMurray Road McMurray Pennsylvania. The tournament began at 1100 a.m. and ended at 230 p.m. After checking the Internet I discovered there are tournaments across the country. Although the McMurray tournament was only a local contest many tournaments lead to a national competition. To find out more about all these tournaments Im going to write to Hasbro Games 443 Shaker Road East Longmeadow Massachusetts 01028.

© Great Source. All rights reserved. (5)

Punctuation Review 2

Here's a challenge. This activity is a review of some of the kinds of punctuation you have studied.

Some of the punctuation has been left out of the following story. First, read the story aloud, then add the needed punctuation. (The number at the end of each line tells you how many punctuation marks you need in that line.)

Last spring, I visited my grandparents birthplace: *(1)*
Fredericksburg, Texas. There are lots of places to go in *(0)*
Fredericksburg Enchanted Rock State Park Fort Martin Scott *(3)*
museums and more. Another place the Plaza of the Presidents *(3)*
honors all the ex presidents who served in World War II. But *(1)*
I want to explain a Fredericksburg tradition—the Easter Fires *(1)*
It dates back to Native American times. *(0)*

White settlers most of the settlers around Fredericksburg *(1)*
were German immigrants built Fredericksburg in an area *(1)*
where Comanche Indians lived. One year, on the night before *(0)*
Easter white and Comanche leaders were having a powwow to *(1)*
decide whether to live in peace or to fight. Small campfires *(0)*
dotted the hillsides around the town One pioneer mother told *(1)*
her children Don't be afraid! The Easter rabbit made the *(2)*

© Great Source. All rights reserved. (5)

fires He is boiling your Easter eggs right now! Of course, the (2)
campfires were Comanche fires the Comanches were waiting (2)
they were waiting as anxiously as the pioneers to hear if a (1)
peace treaty would be made. (0)
Peace was made. The Meusebach-Comanche Treaty of (0)
1847 is one of very few Native American treaties maybe the (1)
only one never broken. The Easter Fires are still lit every (1)
year and a play is performed to retell the dramatic story. (1)

Directions **Add the correct punctuation where it's needed in the following dialogue.**

What are you doing, Frank Jamal asked.

"I'm thinking of titles for my book, song, and movie" said Frank.

Frank, you are only in the fifth grade Jamal said. So, what title do you have I hope it's not something like C's.

"No. My book is about a wolf that gets separated from the pack said Frank. "I'm going to call the book The Lost Wolf Runs."

"Hmm that's not too bad. What are your other titles"

I'll call my movie Standing Tree, said Frank. I'm still working on a song idea.

© Great Source. All rights reserved. (5)

Capitalization 1

You know that the first letter of a sentence is always capitalized. Yet other capitalization rules might not be so obvious. This activity will give you practice capitalizing proper nouns that are geographic terms, proper adjectives, and titles used with names. (See *Write Source* 508.1, 508.3, and 512.1.)

Examples

Proper Nouns That Are Geographic Terms:
My family recently moved here from **Chicago**.
(*Chicago*, the name of a city, is a proper noun.)

Proper Adjectives:
A **Chicago** mayor oversees more people than some state governors do.
(*Chicago* is a proper adjective that modifies *mayor*.)

Titles Used with Names:
For years, Chicagoans kept re-electing **Mayor** Daley.
(*Mayor* is a title connected with a name.)

Find and change the words that should be capitalized. The first sentence has been done for you.

1. Gustavo and I went with aunt Julia to meet governor Flood. (A, G)
2. He came to our town to give a speech about mayor frost.
3. We live in ragener, south carolina.
4. Aunt Julia says mayor Frost is a friend of the governor.
5. So, the governor came to campaign in the capital city, columbia.
6. Once aunt Julia said that the governor would go to mars for mayor Frost.
7. My aunt says the governor wants to go to washington, d.c., not to mars.
8. She thinks governor Flood wants to be the United states president.

© Great Source. All rights reserved. (5)

In the following paragraph, capitalize geographic names. See *Write Source* 512.1.

Yesterday Rod decided to look at a map of the united States to search for interesting places to visit someday. He started by looking at major rivers. He marked the Mississippi river and the missouri River as must-see destinations and thought about taking a raft trip down the Colorado river through the grand canyon. Then Rod noticed some mountain ranges on the map. He thought it would be fun to hike the appalachian mountains in the East and climb some cliffs in the rocky mountains in the West. He knew he wanted to see the volcanoes of the Cascade mountains. Rod's father had a friend who had just hiked through death valley. Rod wasn't sure he wanted to do that, but he did want to see a desert. Finally, Rod wrote down names of large bodies of water. Floating in great Salt lake sounded like fun. Body surfing in the pacific ocean was also one of Rod's long-time dreams. Rod hoped he could find some friends to paddle canoes with him along the shore of Lake superior in minnesota. When Rod finished his wish list, he realized it might take many years to accomplish all of his travel goals.

The Next Step **Write several sentences about famous places you would like to visit. Be sure to properly capitalize your words.**

© Great Source. All rights reserved. (5)

Capitalization 2

Write Source lists many rules for capitalization. In this activity, you'll need to use just a few of those rules. (See pages 508–514.)

Examples

My father can speak **German**.

He is a member of the **Knights of Columbus**.

Each sentence below contains several capitalization errors. Some words and phrases that *should* be capitalized are not; some words and phrases that *should not* be capitalized are. Make the needed corrections. The first sentence has been done for you.

g K W W W

1. My Grandfather fought in the korean war and in world war II.
2. In history class, we're studying the revolutionary war and about the first President of the United States.
3. The league of nations was replaced by the united nations.
4. I've seen the California angels play Baseball in Anaheim Stadium.
5. The most common religion in japan is buddhism.
6. Our puerto rican neighbors speak spanish at home.
7. Most people prefer either dannon or yoplait yogurt.
8. Jay got a McDonald's chicken salad and a cup of wendy's chili.
9. Jonathan is jewish, and his family celebrates hanukkah.
10. Jamila, who is from kenya, knows how to speak swahili.

© Great Source. All rights reserved. (5)

The Next Step **Choose any four of the rules for capitalization shown on *Write Source* pages 508–514. Then write four sentences. Each one of your sentences should use a different rule, but don't capitalize the words that are affected by the rule. Trade with a partner and correct each other's sentences. Be ready to explain the rules you used to make the corrections.**

1. ______________________________

2. ______________________________

3. ______________________________

4. ______________________________

© Great Source. All rights reserved. (5)

Plurals 1

There are rules for making **plurals**. (See *Write Source* pages 516 and 518.)

Examples

pony ➜ ponies
ash ➜ ashes
class ➜ classes
taco ➜ tacos

Directions **Change each word into its plural form. Use the rules explained in *Write Source*.**

1. guess ______________
2. potato ______________
3. puppy ______________
4. lunch ______________
5. tomato ______________
6. candy ______________
7. bush ______________
8. piano ______________
9. key ______________
10. box ______________

The Next Step **Now develop a "List Poem" using as many of the plural words above as possible. (See the model on *Write Source* page 317.)**

____

____

____

____

____

© Great Source. All rights reserved. (5)

Plurals 2

This activity gives you more practice with plurals. (Use *Write Source* pages 516 and 518 to help you.)

Examples

spoonful ➜ spoonfuls
half ➜ halves
justice of the peace ➜ justices of the peace
pulley ➜ pulleys

Directions **Write the plural form of each word below.**

1. life ____________
2. brother-in-law ____________
3. stepmother ____________
4. mouthful ____________
5. roof ____________
6. fly ____________
7. radio ____________
8. fox ____________
9. mosquito ____________
10. woman ____________
11. wolf ____________
12. sheep ____________

The Next Step **Write some silly sentences using all the plurals above that name animals.**

____

____

____

____

____

© Great Source. All rights reserved. (5)

Abbreviations

An **abbreviation** is a shorter way to write a word or a phrase—a shortcut! (*Write Source* pages 520 and 522 explain abbreviations and give examples.)

Examples

Dr. Bob
(Dr. = Doctor)

1125 Oak Tree Ln.
(Ln. = Lane)

Below are some abbreviations that are often used in writing addresses and times. Match each abbreviation to the word or phrase it stands for.

______	1. St.	a.	Highway
______	2. Pkwy.	b.	Terrace
______	3. p.m.	c.	ante meridiem (before noon)
______	4. WY	d.	Court
______	5. N.	e.	Parkway
______	6. Dr.	f.	post meridiem (after noon)
______	7. Sta.	g.	Heights
______	8. Hwy.	h.	North
______	9. Ave.	i.	Wyoming
______	10. Expy.	j.	Street
______	11. Terr.	k.	Drive
______	12. Ct.	l.	Station
______	13. a.m.	m.	Avenue
______	14. Hts.	n.	Expressway

© Great Source. All rights reserved. (5)

Directions **Some other common abbreviations are listed below. Match each abbreviation to the word or phrase it stands for.**

______ **1.** lb.	**a.** doctor of medicine
______ **2.** oz.	**b.** pound
______ **3.** etc.	**c.** paid
______ **4.** pd.	**d.** ounce
______ **5.** M.D.	**e.** mistress
______ **6.** Ms.	**f.** blend of Miss and Mrs.
______ **7.** Mrs.	**g.** et cetera (and so forth)

The Next Step **Now choose a few of the address abbreviations from the matching lists on the previous page and use them in an address you would find at the top of a letter. (See *Write Source* page 522 for more information.)**

© Great Source. All rights reserved. (5)

Numbers 1

This activity gives you practice using **numbers** in your writing. See *Write Source* page 524. It explains when to write numbers as numerals and when to write them as words.

Example

Twelve of us turned to chapter 5, but four students opened their books to page 5.

In the exercise below, some of the numbers need to be changed to numerals, some need to be made into words, and some should be left alone. Refer to the rules on *Write Source* page 524 for additional information and then make your changes. The first sentence has been done for you.

1. There are ~~eleven~~ *11* parts in the school play.
2. 10 people are needed to sing in the chorus.
3. In the play, there are two children who are ten and fifteen years old; all the other characters are adults.
4. 30 of us who are involved with the play will sell tickets.
5. This hilarious comedy has 5 acts and one intermission.
6. If we sell tickets, we'll have to sell fifty tickets to pay for the costumes.
7. We could sell small bags of popcorn for seventy-five ¢ each, if two or three people would agree to sell them.
8. We plan to perform the play on February seven in the evening.
9. 2 afternoon performances are planned for the weekend.

© Great Source. All rights reserved. (5)

Numbers 2

This activity gives you more practice using numbers in sentences. (See *Write Source* page 524 for more information.)

Example

On May 30, five teachers did a short skit.

In the sentences below, correct the numbers by changing some into numerals and some into words. Then, on the line below each sentence, explain why you made the corrections you made. The first sentence has been done for you.

1. The population of our city is ~~one point three~~ 1.3 million.

   Decimals are written as numerals.

2. Our pie chart showed that only eight percent of our class had the flu.

   ____

3. Read chapters one and two, which include pages one through ten.

   ____

4. We voted sixteen to nine to get an aquarium.

   ____

5. 3 of us brought money to help pay for the aquarium, fish, and food.

   ____

6. My birthday party will be Saturday, May six.

   ____

© Great Source. All rights reserved. (5)

Becoming a Better Speller

Making up sayings and acrostics can help you remember the spellings of difficult words.

Examples

Use familiar words:
conscience = con + science

Make up an acrostic (funny sentence):
through = Tim had red, orange, ugly, giant hives.

Try writing sayings or acrostics for four words that give you trouble from the list beginning on *Write Source* page 532. An example has been done for you.

1. *Their, there, and they're all begin with "the."*

2. ______________________________

3. ______________________________

4. ______________________________

5. ______________________________

© Great Source. All rights reserved. (5)

Proofreading Practice

After revising your writing assignments, be sure to check for spelling errors. (See *Write Source* pages 528 and 532–535.)

In the following story, label the underlined words "C" for correct, or cross out the word and write the correct spelling above. The first one has been done for you.

Last ~~Saterday~~ Saturday, we had an advencher. Immediately after lunch, we rode to the woods to climb our faverite old maple tree. We had all climbed the tree befour, but this time we desided to see who coud climb to the highest hieght. Ron climbed even higher than any one else, but it was Rita who was the champyon of this race. Unforchunately, she coudn't get down! She didn't realize how high up in that tree she was, untill she looked down. Then she panicked. She kept clinging to the branch she was on, even tho she was geting tired. Ron rode straigt back to his house, and his dad called the fire department. An enormus fire engine, with an extension lader and with sirens screaming, rushed to Rita's aid. Despite the excitment, we all learned an importent lesson.

© Great Source. All rights reserved. (5)

Spelling Rules 1

Use the basic spelling rules found on *Write Source* page 528 to help you spell *ie* and *ei* words correctly.

Circle the correctly spelled word in each of the pairs below.

1. foreign, foriegn
2. piece, peice
3. cheif, chief
4. weigh, wiegh
5. neice, niece
6. relieve, releive
7. weird, wierd
8. recieve, receive
9. acheive, achieve
10. science, sceince
11. theif, thief
12. height, hieght

Directions

In the following sentences, cross out any misspelled word. Write the correct spelling above the word.

1. Hank and Joe brought thier baseball gloves to the game.
2. The two boys hoped freinds would see them on TV.
3. Neither boy had ever been to a professional baseball game.
4. The two couldn't beleive that they had such good seats.
5. Hank decided to reveiw the lineup for the home team.
6. His favorite player actually grew up in Hank's nieghborhood.

© Great Source. All rights reserved. (5)

Spelling Rules 2

Use the silent *e* rule to correctly spell words with suffixes added. If a word ends with a silent *e*, drop the *e* before adding a suffix (ending) that begins with a vowel.

Examples

Josie likes **creating** (create + ing) computer screen savers.

She is **careful** (care + ful) to save her changes.

Directions **Add the suffix indicated to each of the following words.**

1. advise + ing ____________________
2. hope + ful ____________________
3. achieve + able ____________________
4. state + ment ____________________
5. relate + ing ____________________
6. care + ing ____________________
7. continue + al ____________________
8. create + ive ____________________
9. advise + ment ____________________
10. hope + ing ____________________

The Next Step **Write a sentence for each of the following words: *hope* + *ful*, *judge* + *ing*, *create* + *ion*. (Remember to correctly spell the new words.)**

© Great Source. All rights reserved. (5)

Spelling Rules 3

Words ending in *y* can be tricky to spell. (See *Write Source* 528.3.)

Examples

toy ➜ toys

fly ➜ flies ➜ flying

In the following sentences, correct the misspelled words. The first one has been done for you.

1. Every day Jim ~~trys~~ *tries* to jump over the creek behind the school.
2. The boies are going to play baseball later this afternoon.
3. Emily cryed for joy when she saw her new bike.
4. Jezreel's new puppy is very plaiful.
5. Five ladys and six men from the school board will tour the new school.
6. The principal gave the janitor a new set of keyes.
7. Several countys in the state may build fitness centers.
8. Our neighborhood has five alleyes.
9. Jane keeps two diarys. One is about school, and one is about home.
10. This test will be offered during the next three daies.

The Next Step **Write a sentence using each of the following words in its plural form: *journey, anniversary, Friday,* and *library.***

© Great Source. All rights reserved. (5)

Spelling Rules 4

Words ending in a consonant need special attention. (See *Write Source* 528.4.)

Correct any misspelled words that are underlined in the paragraph below. The first one has been done for you.

Both boys and girls know that batting bating practice is very important. They know that practice is just a beginning for them. With practice, they will get better at spoting a good pitch and hiting the ball. They also know listenning to the coach is important. Some coaches think players should be attackking the ball all the time. Those coaches must be thinkking such a strategy will score runs. The truth is that a batter must choose wisely which pitch to hit. When a ball is bunted, batters have other special concerns. To send the ball climbbing into the sky, a batter has to see a good pitch coming, swing well, and hit the ball solidly. Batters soon learn they are guardding the plate. Once boys and girls learn to hit the ball, they will be beging to bat all the time.

© Great Source. All rights reserved. (5)

Spelling Review 1

Look at the underlined words in the following story. Cross out the misspelled words and write the correct spellings above. If a word is spelled correctly, write "C" above it.

One September afternoon, Jutta and I quickly changed into old cloths and headed to our freinds' trout pond. Once there, we tackled the easy job of neting 10 trout from the holding tank for our supper that night. Then our friends Karl and Bert usd a rowboat to pull a huge fishnet across the pond. Jutta kept the fish busy by tossing food pellets out in front of the net. With Karl on one side and Bert on the other, they began draging the net toward shore. There, Jutta and I neted the churning, thrashhing fish. Niether of us could believe it—150 trout! Our friends would have a freezer full of fish for the winter. Finaly, we moved all the fish into the large holdding tank. Meanwhile, Karl's mother had finished cleaning the 10 trout and seasoning them for the grill. By then we were all geting hungry and impatient for supper.

© Great Source. All rights reserved. (5)

Spelling Review 2

Correct the misspelled words in the paragraph below. The first one has been done for you.

1. Another name for huge thunderstorm ~~cloudes~~ *clouds* is cumulonimbus.
2. One little boy I know crys when he sees that kind of cloud.
3. The lightning, thunder, and big raindropes frighten him.
4. The highhest clouds, known as cirrus, can be more then eight miles above the earth.
5. A cumulonimbus cloud may be thousandes of feet tall.
6. Scientists can estimate how much a cloud wieghs.
7. Fog is a cloud that is moveing slowly across the ground or just standing still.
8. Hopeing to see better in fog, drivers sometimes use yellow lights.
9. Clouds can cover the sky for several daies.
10. Spoting a tornado in a thundercloud is not always easy to do.
11. The freezeing level for clouds is about six and a half miles above the ground.
12. Above that hieght, clouds are made up of ice crystals.
13. Freindly looking cumulus clouds mean fair weather.

© Great Source. All rights reserved. (5)

Using the Right Word 1

Write Source lists many commonly misused words. (See page 536.)

Examples

An iguana is one type of lizard.
A llama has valuable wool.

Mom will accept no pets in the house except her cat.

Abe Lincoln read aloud.
Scruffy is not allowed on the couch.

Do you have a lot of homework?

I'm already finished eating.
Tim is all ready for the game.

Cross out any underlined word that is incorrect and write the correct word above. Do not change any correct words.

In 1849, an brave pioneer family, the Rikers, began a long trip to Oregon. Janette, her two brothers, and her father thought they were already for their journey. However, in Montana, the Riker men went hunting one day and never returned. Janette, who hadn't been aloud to go on the hunt, was left alone in the wilderness—except for the family's ox. The weather was already cold, and Janette had to except the fact that she couldn't cross the Rocky Mountains by herself. Amazingly, she built a hut, chopped alot of wood for making fires, and even killed the ox for meat. With wild animals outside her door, Janette must have talked allowed to herself in her tiny home. In the spring, some Native Americans found Janette alive and took her to Oregon.

© Great Source. All rights reserved. (5)

Using the Right Word 2

Review the following word pairs and see *Write Source* pages 544 and 546.

Examples

There's a **hole** in my sock.
Dad can eat a **whole** pizza!

We're leaving in one **hour**.
Our lunches are packed.

It's a good book.
Its cover is interesting.

I **knew** all the answers.
Here's a **new** box of crayons.

Tie a tight **knot**.
That's **not** tight enough.

Lay your books down.
Mom needs to **lie** down.

Lead is a metal.
Lead the exercises today.
I **led** them yesterday.

Directions Write the correct choice on the line above each set of parentheses.

1. European settlers entered a whole ____________ *(knew, new)* world when they came to America. They ____________ *(knew, new)* that life would ____________ *(knot, not)* be easy.

2. Native Americans told ____________ *(hour, our)* earliest forefathers to put a small fish in the ____________ *(hole, whole)* with the seeds when planting corn. This idea usually ____________ *(lead, led)* to a bigger harvest.

3. Pioneer women spent ____________ *(hours, ours)* making clothing.

4. Rope making and ____________ *(not, knot)* tying were also important pioneer skills.

5. Pioneers' dishes made of pewter contained tin and ____________ *(led, lead)*.

6. ____________ *(Its, It's)* easy to see why pioneers had many skills.

7. Children would ____________ *(lay, lie)* quilts on top of corn-shuck mattresses and ____________ *(lay, lie)* down to sleep.

© Great Source. All rights reserved. (5)

Using the Right Word 3

Be sure you use the right words. (See *Write Source* pages 554 and 556.)

Examples

Don't **waste** food.
Tie the scarf around your **waist**.

Where are you going?
Don't **wear** your hat indoors.

Decide **whether** to walk or ride.
The **weather** is hot.

That's the boy **who** runs fast.
Dry the clothes **that** are wet.
The shirt, **which** is new, is ripped.

Who made this?
For **whom** did you make it?

You're shivering.
Your lips are blue.

Whose books are these?
Who's coming to dinner?

Cross out any underlined word that is incorrect and write the correct word above. Do not change any correct words.

If your going hiking, remember to take along you're map and a compass. The map can tell you wear you are, and a compass can show you weather you are headed in the right direction. Don't waist energy carrying unnecessary stuff. Take plenty of water and nutritious snacks, which will give you extra energy. Check the whether forecast so that you know what to where. If it's warm at first, tie a jacket around you're waste and wear it when the temperature drops. Always expect the unexpected. Someone who's compass is broken can tell his or her direction by the sun and the stars, or by how moss grows on trees. Will you be a hiker whose prepared on the trail, or one whom ends up hungry, cold, and lost? It's up to you.

© Great Source. All rights reserved. (5)

Using the Right Word 4

Many words are commonly misused. (See *Write Source* pages 550 and 552.)

Examples

Raise the flag.
The sun's **rays** are hot.

The answer is **right**.
Write me a note.

We **rowed** the boat.
Mom **rode** on a motorcycle!
The **road** is icy.

You **seem** tired.
The **seam** is ripped open.

Sit next to me.
Just **set** the glass there.

Mom will **sew** the seam.
We will **sow** corn seeds.
Water plants **so** they'll grow.

The artists painted a winter **scene**.
Have you **seen** my glasses?

Write the correct choice above each set of parentheses in the following paragraph.

Grandpa's farm made a perfect country __________ *(seen, scene)* as we arrived for our visit. The sun's __________ *(rays, raise)* made us squint as we turned up the bumpy dirt __________ *(rode, road)* to the house. Grandpa knew everything, it __________ *(seemed, seamed)* to us. He knew when to __________ *(sew, sow, so)* his fields and when to __________ *(set, sit)* on the porch, rocking. That's when we'd __________ *(set, sit)* our chairs close to his and listen to his stories. "Why, I __________ *(rode, road)* a horse five miles to school! Sometimes, she'd try to buck me off __________ *(sew, sow, so)* she could run to the warm barn. Yes, I learned to read and __________ *(rite, write, right)* while shivering." After hearing the stories, we __________ *(rode, road, rowed)* the old boat in the pond. Grandpa told us what crops he used to __________ *(rays, raise)*.

© Great Source. All rights reserved. (5)

Using the Right Word 5

Check the list of commonly misused words in *Write Source* (see pages 548 and 550).

Examples

Pain hurts.
The pane of glass broke.

The past is over.
I passed the runner.

Our principal teaches sometimes.
The Golden Rule is a fine principle.

Find a pair of socks.
Eat this ripe pear.
Let's pare the apples.

The plane flew overhead.
Dad likes plain food.

War is the opposite of peace.
Have a piece of melon.

Replace any underlined word that is incorrect with the correct word. The first one has been done for you.

1. The ~~principle~~ *principal* of our school is a Boy Scout leader. At each hobby fair in the passed, Mr. Fuhrman had an exhibit explaining the principal of natural navigation. His directions for finding one's way by using a stick as a sundial were very plane. This year, he will tell us how to make a pare of moccasins out of birch bark.

2. There will be no piece around Ms. Keller's baking booth. Last year, no one passed that exhibit without tasting a peace of fruit pizza. She also will be showing how to pare all sorts of fruit, including pears.

3. Then there's the gym teacher's "no pane, no gain" weight-lifting booth. He'll show us how to get a pear of biceps even a bodybuilder would envy.

4. The art teacher's model plain has pilots behind a tiny pain of plastic.

© Great Source. All rights reserved. (5)

Using the Right Word 6

Review the commonly misused words on *Write Source* pages 542 and 544.

Examples

He **doesn't** dance.
We **don't** dance.

My paper has **fewer** errors today. I have **less** homework than you do.

You look **good** in blue.
She sings **well**.

The **heel** of my foot is sore.
I wish it would **heal**.

Come **here**.
Did you **hear** me?

Directions **Write the correct choice on the line above each set of parentheses.**

1. The United States ____________ have a monopoly on tornadoes.
   (doesn't, don't)
2. Britain has ____________ twisters per year, but it's a smaller country.
   (fewer, less)
3. Scientists find that people in the United States are ____________ likely
   (less, fewer)
   to experience a tornado than people in Britain.
4. Low pressure and rapidly rising warm air create a ____________
   (good, well)
   chance for a damaging funnel of wind to form.
5. So ____________ ignore a tornado warning.
   (doesn't, don't)
6. If you ever ____________ a tornado siren, you would do ____________
   (here, hear) *(good, well)*
   to take cover immediately.
7. A serious tornado causes ____________ damage than a hurricane does.
   (fewer, less)
8. ____________ in this country, tornadoes are common in the Midwest.
   (Hear, Here)
9. After damaging storms, injured people may take time to ____________.
   (heel, heal)

© Great Source. All rights reserved. (5)

Using the Right Word 7

Learn to use the following words correctly in your writing. (See *Write Source* pages 538 and 540.)

Examples

The bear growled.
Amy's bare legs were cold.

The oak board is strong.
Sue is bored with TV.

The bike's brake sticks.
Break the cookie in half.

Please bring me the shovel.
Then take this rake to Jim.

Just walk by the store.
Don't buy another CD.

I can run fast.
May I have more cake?

Cross out any underlined word that is used incorrectly and write the correct word above it.

Although brown bears are the most common bears on earth, the polar bare may survive farther north in the harsh ice and snow of the Arctic. Under its thick, white fur, the animal's bare skin is black. The sun's rays are absorbed buy the dark skin. The polar bear's fur, made up of hollow hairs, traps the warmth. Buy its huge size, you may have guessed this bear's other secret to keeping warm—a thick layer of fat. A polar bear's keen sense of smell can bring it to prey as far away as 30 miles! A bear waiting next to a hole in the ice may look board or lazy, as it waits for nature to take a seal for supper. When the ice begins to brake up in the spring, a bare may end up adrift on an ice floe. This is no problem because polar bears are great swimmers.

© Great Source. All rights reserved. (5)

Using the Right Word 8

Write Source offers lists of commonly misused words (see pages 552 and 554).

Examples

Birds soar above us.
My ankle is sore.

Something stationary doesn't move.
I have a box of pretty stationery.

The I-beam is made of steel.
Scruffy likes to steal Boots' food.

Then the car stalled.
Cake tastes better than squash.

He threw the ball.
Walk through the park.

It's their turn. They're up to bat.
See the pitcher over there.

Cross out any underlined word that is incorrect. Write the correct word above it. Do not change any correct words.

1. Some people ride stationery bikes in there homes. Others visit health clubs where their involved in activities that make muscles soar at first but make them strong as steal later.

2. When people hit the ski slopes, they're spirits sore as they swish downhill with the wind in there faces. Than they say that they like skiing better then working out in a gym.

3. Their is a problem with the exercise craze, however, and that is injury. Doctors see many patients these days who through out there backs or dislocated they're knees while trying to get fit.

4. My mom stays fit by chasing my little brother around all day, and when she's threw with that, she makes a cup of tea. Than she reads, stamps her own cards and stationary, or plays the piano.

© Great Source. All rights reserved. (5)

Using the Right Word 9

Use the right words. (See *Write Source* pages 540 and 542.)

Examples

The capital of Maine is Augusta.
Many capitol buildings have domes.

Please close the window.
Old clothes are comfortable.

Don't dye your hair.
Amy hopes her goldfish doesn't die.

A desert gets little rain.
The dessert is chocolate.

The math course is hard.
Coarse means "rough".

Don't do that.
The book is due today.
Insects drink dew.

Roses have a popular scent.
I sent Dad some flowers.
This candy cost one cent!

Cross out any underlined word that is incorrect. Write the correct word above it. Do not change any correct words.

In our social studies coarse last year, we studied our state's history. We visited the capital building in our capitol city and a pioneer museum. At this living-history museum, we visited several houses, and the sent of prairie flowers was in the air. A woman dressed in old-fashioned close was making a pudding over an open fire for desert. She told us how homemakers in 1845 had to due things differently than today. Other women were using walnuts to die yarn to weave into cloth. By noon, the do on the fields had dried, and the sun was hot. We had to walk everywhere, and the dusty roads felt like crossing a dessert. Later, we bought postcards for 25 sents and scent them to friends.

© Great Source. All rights reserved. (5)

Using the Right Word 10

Check the list of commonly misused words found in *Write Source.* (See pages 546 and 548).

Examples

I can learn to swim.
Midge will teach me.

Don't lose your gloves.
The pants are too loose.

Silver is a precious metal.
Jason earned a gold medal.

A minor cannot vote.
That's a minor problem.
The miner works underground.

The boat is missing an oar.
Sit here or there.
Iron ore is heavy.

Directions **Write the correct choice on the line above each set of parentheses below.**

1. "What did you ____________ today?" Mom asked us at the dinner table.
(learn, teach)

2. We shared ____________ details ____________ facts from our lessons.
(miner, minor) *(or, ore, oar)*

3. It helps you understand something if you ____________ it to someone else.
(learn, teach)

4. A gold ____________ in California in 1849 was called a "forty-niner."
(minor, miner)

5. ____________ panned gold from streams. They swirled ____________
(Minors, Miners) *(loose, lose)*
gravel in water until only gold flakes, grains, or nuggets remained.

6. Usually, gold ____________ is found in combination with other
(medal, metal)
minerals. The combination is called gold ____________.
(or, ore, oar)

7. An Olympic ____________ is either gold, silver, or bronze.
(metal, medal)

8. You use a paddle in a canoe and an ____________ in a rowboat.
(or, ore, oar)

9. Our ginkgo tree may ____________ all of its leaves overnight.
(loose, lose)

10. A ____________ must be with an adult to attend certain movies.
(miner, minor)

© Great Source. All rights reserved. (5)

Using the Right Word Review

This activity reviews some of the commonly misused words you have practiced.

Choose the correct word in parentheses to fill in each blank in the sentences below. Be sure to capitalize the first word in a sentence. The first sentence has been done for you.

1. ___You're___ going to get wet without ___your___ umbrella. *(your, you're)*
2. __________ going to England to visit __________ uncle who lives __________. *(their, there, they're)*
3. __________ time to give the bird __________ medicine. *(its, it's)*
4. Our teacher doesn't __________ late homework __________ when a student is sick. *(accept, except)*
5. __________ sister said __________ going shopping. *(your, you're)*
6. Cherie __________ she needed a __________ notebook. *(knew, new)*
7. __________ the books on my desk, please. *(lay, lie)*
8. Joe told us that __________ of people saw the giant meteor last night *(alot, a lot)*.
9. There are so many __________ piled in my closet that I can't __________ the door. *(close, clothes)*
10. I can go to the movie because I have __________ finished my homework. *(already, all ready)*

© Great Source. All rights reserved. (5)

11. If you make a ____________ in your sleeve, you'll ruin your ____________ sweater. *(hole, whole)*

12. If I ____________ to knit, I can ____________ you how to make a scarf. *(learn, teach)*

13. When the ____________ splattered all over her, Carla thought she would ____________ of embarrassment. *(die, dye)*

14. I planned to write ____________ letter, ____________ editorial. *(a, an)*

The Next Step **Write a sentence for each pair of words below. Be sure to use the words correctly.**

1. led, lead ____

____

____

2. threw, through ____

____

____

3. buy, by ____

____

____

© Great Source. All rights reserved. (5)

Sentence Activities

The activities in this section cover three important areas: (1) the basic parts of sentences, (2) common sentence errors, and (3) ways to add variety to sentences. Most activities contain a main practice part, in which you review, combine, or analyze sentences. In addition, The Next Step activities give you follow-up practice with certain skills.

Sentence Basics	**77**
Sentence Problems	**85**
Sentence Variety	**103**

Simple Subjects and Predicates

What are the basic parts that every sentence must have? If you answered a **subject** and a **verb**, you are right. In the examples below, the subject is underlined once and the verb twice. (See pages 432–434, 560, and 562 in *Write Source* for more information.)

Examples

Fish swim in the ocean.

Birds fly in the sky.

Read the five sentences below. Find the subject in each sentence. Then rewrite the sentences, changing the subject. The new subject can be anything you choose, as long as it makes a correct sentence. Circle your new subjects. The first one has been done for you.

1. Can fish fly?

   Can a dog fly?

2. The flying fish doesn't really fly.

   ____

3. Like a glider, the flying fish soars through the air.

   ____

4. Ducks swim in lakes and ponds.

   ____

5. Do ducks fly south for the winter?

   ____

© Great Source. All rights reserved. (5)

Read the same five sentences taken from the previous exercise and rewrite the sentences again. This time change the verb instead of the subject. Circle your new verbs.

1. Can fish fly?

____

2. The flying fish doesn't really fly.

____

3. Like a glider, the flying fish soars through the air.

____

4. Ducks swim in lakes and ponds.

____

5. Do ducks fly south for the winter?

____

The Next Step **Write four sentences about your favorite time of the year. Circle the simple subject and underline the simple predicate.**

© Great Source. All rights reserved. (5)

Compound Subjects and Predicates

A sentence may have more than one subject (called a **compound subject**) or more than one predicate (called a **compound predicate**). In fact, a sentence may even have both a compound subject and a compound predicate. (See *Write Source* page 435, 560.4, and 562.4.)

Examples

Compound Subject: My sister and her friend went to a movie.

Compound Predicate: They ate popcorn and drank soda.

Rewrite each of the following sentences two times. The first time, change the sentence so that it has a compound subject. The second time, change the sentence so that it has a compound predicate. The first one has been done for you.

1. Tracy moved to Arizona.

   Compound Subject: Tracy and Teddi moved to Arizona.

   Compound Predicate: Tracy moved to Arizona and started school.

2. Tracy's grandmother lives there.

   Compound Subject: ______________________________

   ____

   Compound Predicate: ______________________________

   ____

© Great Source. All rights reserved. (5)

3. Tracy wrote us a letter.

Compound Subject: ______________________________

____

Compound Predicate: ______________________________

____

4. Tracy goes swimming every day.

Compound Subject: ______________________________

____

Compound Predicate: ______________________________

____

The Next Step **Write one sentence that has a compound subject, one sentence that has a compound predicate, and one sentence that has both. Your sentences can be about Tracy and her family in Arizona, or about anything you like.**

1. *Compound Subject:* ______________________________

____

2. *Compound Predicate:* ______________________________

____

3. *Compound Subject and Compound Predicate:* ______________________________

____

____

© Great Source. All rights reserved. (5)

Clauses

A **clause** is a group of related words that has both a subject and a predicate. An **independent clause** expresses a complete thought and can stand alone as a sentence. A **dependent clause** does not express a complete thought and cannot stand alone. (See *Write Source* page 564.)

Examples

Independent Clause: Our old VCR worked.

Dependent Clause: After we fixed the remote control

On the line before each clause, write "D" if it is a dependent clause and "I" if it is an independent clause. Add correct end punctuation for each independent clause. The first one has been done for you.

___I___ 1. We got a new VCR.

______ 2. When we lost the remote control

______ 3. After Max put his peanut butter sandwich in it

______ 4. Max is only three

______ 5. Since the sandwich was in there

______ 6. A million ants crawled into the VCR

______ 7. When my dad found out

______ 8. Until Max gets older

______ 9. The new VCR sits on a high shelf

______ 10. Although Max broke the VCR

______ 11. Mom says Max is creative

© Great Source. All rights reserved. (5)

Directions Make each dependent clause on the previous page into a complete sentence. To do this, add an independent clause. The first one has been done for you.

1. *When we lost the remote control, we didn't know how to start the VCR.*

2. ______________________________

3. ______________________________

4. ______________________________

5. ______________________________

6. ______________________________

The Next Step Write two sentences with a dependent clause at the beginning and two sentences with a dependent clause at the end. Underline the dependent clauses.

© Great Source. All rights reserved. (5)

Prepositional Phrases

A **prepositional phrase** includes a preposition, the object of the preposition, and any describing words that come in between. (For a list of prepositions, see *Write Source* page 598.)

Examples

He ran through the doorway.
(This prepositional phrase includes the preposition *through*, the object *doorway*, and the article *the*.)

Without a doubt, they had the flu.

In the sentences below, circle each preposition, and underline each prepositional phrase. The number of phrases is given in parentheses. The first sentence has been done for you.

1. David made a valentine for his mom. *(1)*
2. He made it in the shape of a heart on red paper. *(3)*
3. It had a picture of flowers on the front. *(2)*
4. David wrote a poem inside the card. *(1)*
5. It was about all the things his mom does for him. *(2)*
6. He signed his name beneath the poem and put the card in an envelope. *(2)*
7. He gave it to his mom after school. *(2)*
8. She told everyone about the card she got from David. *(2)*
9. She took the card to work and put it on her desk. *(2)*

© Great Source. All rights reserved. (5)

Directions **Use the prepositional phrases listed below to fill in the blanks of the story.**

in the nets	with each other	in the ocean	into a tight circle
to the ocean's surface	from trainers	in front of ships	along the bottom
into the circling fish	near people	into the air	Around the world

Dolphins are some of the most graceful animals that live __________________. They can swim as fast as 25 miles per hour and sometimes leap high __________________. Dolphins have been seen swimming __________________ to catch the bow wave. They work together to force fish __________________. The dolphins then take turns dashing __________________. Because dolphins are mammals, they have to swim __________________ to breathe. Sharks are their biggest enemies in the water.

__________________, fishing vessels are a real danger. These boats sometimes use huge nets that drag __________________ of the ocean. Dolphins can get caught __________________. Fortunately, newer net designs have helped dolphins escape. Dolphins are very curious and like to be __________________. Dolphins communicate __________________ using clicks, chirps, and actions. They also seem to understand instructions __________________. One day, scientists hope to communicate with these creatures.

© Great Source. All rights reserved. (5)

Sentence Fragments 1

The following activity gives you practice correcting one kind of sentence error: **sentence fragments.** A fragment is a group of words that is missing a subject, a predicate (verb), or both. It does not express a complete thought. (See *Write Source* page 436.)

Examples

Sentence Fragments:

Lives at the zoo. (missing a subject)

The animals in that cage. (missing a predicate)

Roaming around. (missing a subject and a predicate)

Directions

On each line below, put an "S" if the words that follow are a sentence, or an "F" if they are a fragment. For each fragment, figure out what is missing—the subject, the verb, or both—and write that word on the line to the right of the fragment. The first fragment has been marked for you.

F 1. A baby alligator to our science class. verb

_____ 2. Brought it from the zoo. _____

_____ 3. It was only about one foot long. _____

_____ 4. Named her Alice. _____

_____ 5. Was afraid of the alligator. _____

_____ 6. Alice afraid of him, too. _____

_____ 7. Next week, the zookeeper will bring an iguana. _____

_____ 8. Our teacher animals. _____

_____ 9. Animal visits make our class fun. _____

_____ 10. In the afternoon. _____

© Great Source. All rights reserved. (5)

Go back to the fragments on page 85 and make each one into a complete sentence. Add and underline a subject, a verb, or both, whatever is needed. Use correct capitalization and punctuation. The first one has been done for you.

1. *A baby alligator came to our science class.*

2. ______________________________

3. ______________________________

4. ______________________________

5. ______________________________

6. ______________________________

7. ______________________________

The Next Step Write five sentences about your favorite zoo animal. Make sure at least two of the sentences are sentence fragments. Exchange papers with a classmate and rewrite the fragments so that they are complete sentences.

© Great Source. All rights reserved. (5)

Sentence Fragments 2

This activity gives you some practice correcting sentence fragments. (See *Write Source* page 436.)

Examples

Sentence Fragments:

needed help to stand due to polio (missing a subject)

Roosevelt often in a wheelchair (missing a verb)

On each line below, put an "S" if the words that follow are a sentence. Put an "F" if they are a fragment. For each fragment, figure out what is missing—the subject, the verb, or both—and write that word on the line to the right of the fragment. The first one has been done for you.

___F___ 1. Franklin Roosevelt president from 1933 to 1945. ___verb___

_______ 2. Was elected four times. _______

_______ 3. A lot of other things, too. _______

_______ 4. Once, he and his friends sailed to an island. _______

_______ 5. Went there to find buried treasure. _______

_______ 6. Didn't find any treasure. _______

_______ 7. Roosevelt something else, though. _______

_______ 8. Found a nest with four baby birds in it. _______

_______ 9. He became an avid bird-watcher. _______

_______ 10. Enjoyed swimming and sailing with his children. _______

_______ 11. Roosevelt one daughter and five sons. _______

© Great Source. All rights reserved. (5)

Read the following paragraph. All the sentences are fragments. Write in the subject or verb that will complete the sentence using the words listed below. You may use the same word more than once. The first one has been done for you.

Jefferson	helped	had	he
designed	was	liked	sent

Thomas Jefferson ^was president of the United States from 1801–1809. The House of Representatives elected him president in 1801 because he and Aaron Burr the same number of electoral votes. In 1803, bought the Louisiana Territory from France. Jefferson then Louis and Clark to explore the new lands of the Louisiana Purchase. Jefferson interested in knowing what kind of animals lived there and what the land looked like. For many years, tried to keep the country out of the wars going on in Europe. In 1809, retired from public life and went to live at his home, which was known as Monticello. Jefferson this home. He to study many subjects including science, architecture, and music. Wanting to support education, founded the University of Virginia. He to build its first building.

The Next Step **Correct each fragment on page 87 so that it becomes a complete sentence.**

© Great Source. All rights reserved. (5)

Run-On Sentences 1

Write Source explains a sentence error called **run-on sentences**. (See page 437.) You can fix this error by adding end punctuation and a capital letter to split the run-on sentence into two sentences.

Example

Run-On Sentence:
Mark Twain's real name was Samuel Clemens "Mark Twain" was his pen name.

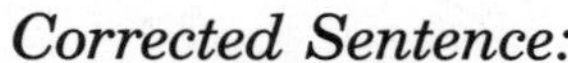

Corrected Sentence:
Mark Twain's real name was Samuel Clemens. "Mark Twain" was his pen name.

Correct the run-on sentences below by dividing them into two sentences. Use correct capitalization and end punctuation in your new sentences. If the sentence is not a run-on sentence, put a check mark next to it. The first sentence has been done for you.

_____ 1. Mark Twain wrote *Tom Sawyer* and *Huckleberry Finn*. He is one of America's most famous authors.

_____ 2. He was born in Missouri he traveled all over the world.

_____ 3. Before he became a writer, Twain was a riverboat pilot.

_____ 4. He worked on steamboats on the Mississippi River until the river was blockaded during the Civil War.

_____ 5. Twain was also a silver miner in Nevada he was a newspaper reporter, too.

_____ 6. Later, he lived in Hartford, Connecticut, with his family.

© Great Source. All rights reserved. (5)

Run-On Sentences 2

A **run-on sentence** can be corrected by adding a comma and a connecting word to make one correct sentence. (See *Write Source* page 437.)

Example

Run-On Sentence:
Grandma Moses lived to be 101 years old she was a centenarian.

Corrected Sentence:
Grandma Moses lived to be 101 years old, so she was a centenarian.

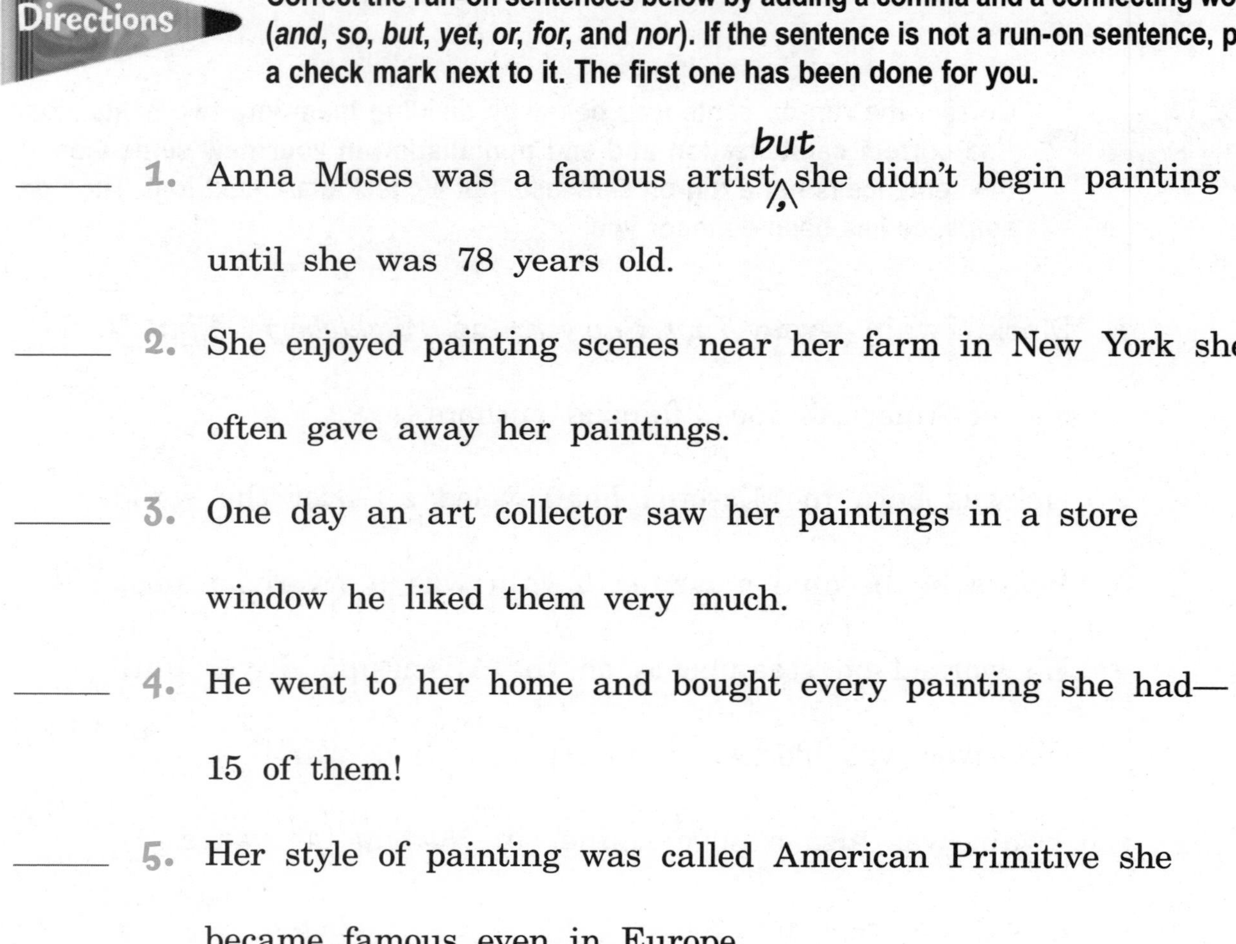

Directions **Correct the run-on sentences below by adding a comma and a connecting word (*and, so, but, yet, or, for,* and *nor*). If the sentence is not a run-on sentence, put a check mark next to it. The first one has been done for you.**

_____ 1. Anna Moses was a famous artist, but she didn't begin painting until she was 78 years old.

_____ 2. She enjoyed painting scenes near her farm in New York she often gave away her paintings.

_____ 3. One day an art collector saw her paintings in a store window he liked them very much.

_____ 4. He went to her home and bought every painting she had—15 of them!

_____ 5. Her style of painting was called American Primitive she became famous even in Europe.

© Great Source. All rights reserved. (5)

Rambling Sentences 1

Write Source explains several different kinds of sentence errors and how to correct them. (See page 437.) This activity gives you practice correcting one kind of sentence error: **rambling sentences**. A rambling sentence happens when you put too many little sentences together with the word *and*.

Below are two rambling sentences. Correct them by dividing them into as many sentences as you think are needed. Cross out the extra *and*'s, capitalize the first word of each sentence, and use the correct end punctuation. The first part of number 1 has been done for you.

1. Our class went to the art museum, and a man who worked there gave us a special tour. ~~and~~ He told us all about the artists, such as when they had lived and he told us that one artist named Vincent van Gogh had cut off his own ear and Raul asked why, and our guide said that nobody knew for sure and Raul thinks that van Gogh didn't know what he was doing.

2. Maria's mom owns a restaurant called Old Mexico and it's near our school and Maria's mom invited our whole class to come to the restaurant for lunch and our teacher said that we could go, so we went today and we all got to have anything we wanted, and almost everybody had two desserts and it was great!

© Great Source. All rights reserved. (5)

Rambling Sentences 2

Below are two more rambling sentences. Correct them by dividing them into as many sentences as you think are needed. Cross out the extra *and*'s, capitalize the first word of each sentence, and use the correct end punctuation.

1. Samantha loves the rain and runs outside whenever it rains sometimes she stands in the rain as droplets splash on her face, and she listens to the raindrops hitting the leaves on the trees Samantha tries to imagine what it would be like to be the size of an ant and she doesn't think it would be much fun to be an ant outside in the rain and she thinks it might even be dangerous, and so she's glad that she isn't an ant.

2. The boys' soccer team played well all year and is going to play in the championship game next week and all the students plan to go to the game and cheer for the team and Benington School has had a soccer team for 20 years, but the school has never had a team get into the play-offs before and the whole town is excited and every one of the players has scored at least one goal this year and made an important defensive play and that means the team's success has been due to a combined team effort.

© Great Source. All rights reserved. (5)

Double Negatives

Do not use two negative words, like *not* and *no,* in the same sentence. *Write Source* page 439 explains **double negatives** and shows how to avoid them.

Example

Immigrants **didn't** have **nowhere** to stay at first. (Change *nowhere* to *anywhere.*)

Correct the double negatives in the following sentences by crossing out or changing the word that is incorrect. If the sentence is correct, put a "C" next to it. The first sentence has been done for you.

_____ 1. A long time ago, people never went ~~nowhere~~ *anywhere* far from home.

_____ 2. There wasn't no reason to leave home.

_____ 3. When Europeans discovered the Americas existed, people began to think about the new land.

_____ 4. Most of these people had never owned no land.

_____ 5. Many years later, poor crops and bad weather caused some people to travel to North and South America to farm.

_____ 6. It was never not easy to clear the land and plant crops.

_____ 7. Many farmers were successful, so others came because they didn't want to be left without no land.

The Next Step **Rewrite two of the sentences above that contain double negatives. Correct them in another way this time.**

© Great Source. All rights reserved. (5)

Sentence Errors Review 1

In this activity, you will practice correcting different kinds of sentence errors.

In the following sentences, there are sentence fragments, run-on sentences, and double negatives. Make the necessary corrections. If the sentence is correct, circle the number.

1. Some classrooms in our school closets for hats and coats.
2. Give tests at least once a week.
3. Joe looked in his backpack, he couldn't find no pencil for the test.
4. My classroom has a tank with three turtles that Arian found and all the students take turns cleaning the tank so that the turtles won't get sick and each day a student is supposed to make sure the turtles are fed.
5. After the turtles were placed in the tank, Rene worried that the turtles wouldn't get no light on weekends.
6. Our brought a light that would hang over the tank.
7. The turtles like to climb on a rock near the light to warm themselves.
8. We that these turtles had to be underwater to swallow their food.
9. The turtles love to eat grasshoppers, but they don't like no spiders.
10. One of the turtles only two inches long.
11. The biggest turtle often sleeps underwater and two other turtles hide in a rock cave and the smallest turtle stays near the other turtles.
12. The whole class watching and caring for the turtles.

© Great Source. All rights reserved. (5)

Sentence Errors Review 2

In this activity, you will practice correcting different kinds of sentence errors.

The paragraph below is full of sentence fragments and run-on sentences. Add the needed words and punctuation to make each sentence complete and correct. The first correction has been done for you.

You probably know that frogs are amphibians. But ‸*here are* some additional facts about frogs. Their eardrums are on the outside of their bodies next to their eyes they can breathe through their skin! Strange creatures. A frog's tongue is attached to its mouth in the front your tongue is attached to the back of your mouth. Is also coated with sticky stuff. Can easily catch insects with it. Most frogs start out as tadpoles some hatch as tiny frogs called froglets. One more fact about frogs. Some frogs *estivate* that means they bury themselves in sand and stay in a sleeplike state when it is hot.

The following paragraph includes some rambling sentences and double negatives. Correct them by breaking them into shorter sentences and crossing out incorrect words.

You can watch frogs change from eggs to tadpoles to frogs. All you have to do is go to a quiet pond or a creek in the spring and find some frogs' eggs and then bring them home and watch what happens. An adult can help you find them. Make sure you

© Great Source. All rights reserved. (5)

bring home only a few frogs' eggs and cover them with some of the water in which you found them and also bring some algae and water plants to use in the water with the eggs. The eggs will become little tadpoles in only about a week and when that happens, you should take most of them back to the pond, and you shouldn't never keep more than one or two and also get some fresh water and plants from the pond. At first tadpoles haven't got no legs. You will see the tadpoles grow back legs first, and then they will grow front legs and their tails will go away, too, and by the way, don't worry if your tadpoles never eat nothing while they are losing their tails. That's normal. Now your tadpoles are frogs and you should take them back to where you found them when they were only eggs because grown frogs need to eat living insects and they also need to live with other frogs. Otherwise the frog life cycle can't not go on.

© Great Source. All rights reserved. (5)

Subject-Verb Agreement 1

One basic rule of writing sentences is that the subject and verb must *agree*. (Sentence agreement is explained on *Write Source* pages 420 and 438.)

Examples

My aunt is from Hawaii.
(*Aunt* and *is* agree because they are both singular.)

Native Americans have their own languages.
(*Native Americans* and *have* agree because they are both plural.)

Directions **Check the following sentences for subject-verb agreement. If the sentence is correct, put a "C" in front of it. If the subject and verb do not agree, correct the verb. The first one has been done for you.**

_______ 1. Americans speaks more than 100 different languages.

_______ 2. Many people moves to the United States from other countries.

_______ 3. They bring their languages with them.

_______ 4. Most immigrants comes from Mexico and Vietnam.

_______ 5. My friend Annie speak Tagalog.

_______ 6. She is from the Philippines.

_______ 7. Jorge and Marta speaks Spanish.

_______ 8. English and Spanish are the most common languages in the United States.

_______ 9. Some native-born Americans speak two languages.

© Great Source. All rights reserved. (5)

Subject-Verb Agreement 2

Subject-verb agreement means that if the subject of a sentence is singular, the verb must be singular, too; if the subject is plural, the verb must be plural. Sometimes you have to read carefully to figure out whether the subject is singular or plural. (See *Write Source* pages 420 and 438.)

Examples

Megan and Kevin are twins.

Kelly is their sister.

In the sentences below, circle the verbs that agree with the subjects. The first one has been done for you.

1. Every summer the kids in my neighborhood *(put, puts)* on a play.
2. Justin and his family *(build, builds)* the stage in their backyard.
3. Isaac or his brother *(is, are)* the director.
4. Charlie and Juanita *(make, makes)* posters and *(sell, sells)* tickets.
5. Carla or her sisters *(is, are)* in charge of costumes.
6. My friend's mom *(help, helps)* with the props.
7. Our parents and my uncle Harry *(provide, provides)* popcorn and soda.
8. Usually my friend *(play, plays)* the lead role.
9. The actors and the director *(practice, practices)* all summer.

© Great Source. All rights reserved. (5)

10. On the last weekend in August, we *(is, are)* finally ready.

11. This year's play, written by Isaac and Sharon, *(is, are)* about Robin Hood.

12. Jared or Scott *(is, are)* sure to play Robin.

13. The whole neighborhood *(is, are)* waiting for opening night.

14. The actors *(is, are)* getting nervous.

15. Five teams of professional actors *(donates, donate)* their time as well.

16. Several families *(has, have)* set up chairs for the audience.

17. The local hardware store *(provide, provides)* the lighting for each performance.

18. This year ID Camera Company *(plans, plan)* to make a DVD of the play.

The Next Step **Imagine that you and your friends are going to put on a play. Write a paragraph telling who would do all the different jobs. Make sure your subjects and verbs agree.**

____

____

____

____

____

____

© Great Source. All rights reserved. (5)

Subject-Verb Agreement 3

Making subjects and verbs agree can be harder when the sentence has a **compound subject**. (Review compound subjects on *Write Source* pages 420 and 438.)

Examples

Luke and Leeann listen to CD's.

Mitchell or the twins ride the scooter.

In some of the following sentences, the subject and verb do not agree. Correct the verbs in those sentences. Put a "C" in front of any correct sentences. The first sentence has been done for you.

_________ 1. My mother or sisters ask~~s~~ me questions in Spanish.

_________ 2. Ricki and Rhoda takes me to the movies.

_________ 3. The teacher or the principal make the announcements.

_________ 4. The first baseman or the shortstop bat first.

_________ 5. My brothers and their dog go to the park.

_________ 6. Rick or his sisters takes the trash out.

_________ 7. My family and my school recycles paper.

_________ 8. My mom or my sisters drive me to school.

_________ 9. My sisters or my mom drive me to school.

The Next Step **Using one of the sentences above as a starting point, write a brief paragraph. Use as many compound subjects as you can. Be sure that your verbs agree.**

© Great Source. All rights reserved. (5)

Subject-Verb Agreement Review 1

This activity gives you more practice with subject-verb agreement. (See *Write Source* pages 420 and 438.)

Some of the underlined verbs below do not agree with their subjects. If the verb does not agree, cross it out and write in the correct verb. If the verb does agree, put a "C" above it.

The students in my class is making an anthology. An anthology is a collection of writings. There is poems, stories, and drawings in our anthology. Every student have one poem or story in the anthology.

Lisa and Serena loves to make books. They or our teacher remind us each day what needs to be done next. Don or the Haring twins are designing the front cover. They are the best artists in our class. Tina and Mark, with help from the teacher, is laying out the pages on the computer. Kerry's parents, who own a print shop, is going to print and bind the books. The class members gets to go to their shop to see how they make the books.

When the books are ready, all the students in the class gets three copies. There is going to be extra copies to sell, too. We hope we can earn the money we need to pay for the paper and ink.

© Great Source. All rights reserved. (5)

Subject-Verb Agreement Review 2

In the following sentences, write the underlined verb in the singular or plural form to match its subject. If the subject and verb agree, write a "C" above the underlined verb.

1. National park rangers now say that some forest fires are good.
2. A forest fire burn away dry leaves and dead branches.
3. Research show that fire actually helps some plants.
4. For example, the lodgepole pine tree have cones that open only after a fire.
5. Burned trees and plants releases nutrients into the soil.
6. During a fire, plants and animals suffer.
7. Months after a fire, new plant growth mean food for wildlife.
8. Nowadays, firefighters does not try to stop every fire.
9. Sometimes, park rangers or firefighters even sets small fires to help prevent big fires.
10. Forests that are protected from fires has only old trees.
11. In old forests, young trees is not able to get sunlight and grow.
12. An older forest are often devastated by diseases and insects.
13. Some scientists think that forest fires help control these problems.
14. No one want a fire, but experts now believe some fires are good.

© Great Source. All rights reserved. (5)

Combining Sentences Using Key Words

You can combine sentences by moving a **key word** from one sentence to another. (See *Write Source* page 445.)

Example

Short Sentences: I lost my book.
It's my math book.

Combined Sentence: I lost my math book.

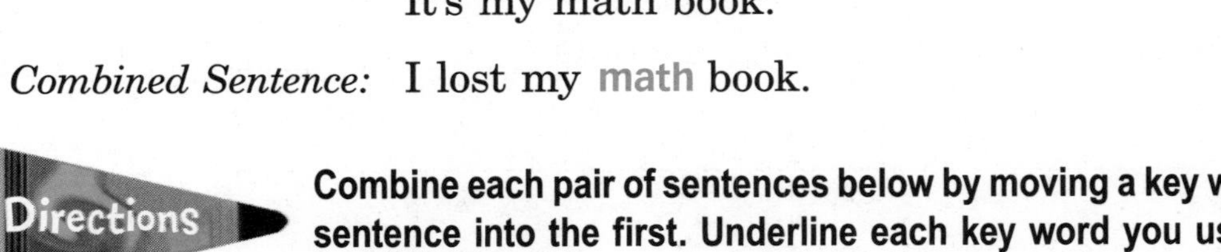

Combine each pair of sentences below by moving a key word from the second sentence into the first. Underline each key word you use. The first one has been done for you.

1. Our teacher found a kitten. It is tiny.

   Our teacher found a tiny kitten.

2. Our classroom computer crashed. It happened yesterday.

   ____

3. My dog snores. He snores loudly.

   ____

4. My friend Willy wrote a story. It's a fantasy.

   ____

5. We're going to the park. We're going there later.

   ____

© Great Source. All rights reserved. (5)

Fill in each blank below with any adjective or adverb that makes sense. Then combine each pair of sentences, using the word you filled in as a key word. The first one has been done for you.

1. Dinah opened the door. She opened it ___slowly___.

   Dinah opened the door slowly.

2. The door creaked. It creaked ______________.

   ____

3. Aunt Millie was wearing a hat. The hat was ______________.

   ____

4. Mason painted his room. He painted it ______________.

   ____

5. Sarah was wearing a costume. The costume was ______________.

   ____

6. The cat purred. It purred ______________.

   ____

7. My mom grows roses. They are ______________.

   ____

8. Our dog barked at the squirrel. Our dog barked ______________.

   ____

9. Five cars are parked in the alley. They are parked ______________.

   ____

© Great Source. All rights reserved. (5)

Combining Sentences with a Series of Words or Phrases 1

You can combine short sentences using a **series of words** or **phrases.** (See *Write Source* page 446.)

Example

Short Sentences: The winters here are too long. They are too cold. They are also too snowy.

Combined Sentence: The winters here are too long, too cold, and too snowy.

Combine each group of sentences below, using a series of words or phrases. The first one has been done for you.

1. The river has steep banks. It has a fast current. It has dangerous falls.

   The river has steep banks, a fast current, and dangerous falls.

2. Last night we heard chirping crickets. We also heard hooting owls. We also heard howling coyotes.

   ____

   ____

3. Dad puts tomatoes in his spaghetti sauce. He also puts in mushrooms. He also puts in onions.

   ____

   ____

4. It was cool in the cave. It was dark. It was damp.

   ____

© Great Source. All rights reserved. (5)

Fill in the blanks below with any words or phrases that make sense. Then combine each group of sentences. The first one has been done for you.

1. Garter snakes are ___small___. They are ___colorful___.
   They are also ___harmless___.
   Garter snakes are small, colorful, and harmless.

2. Elephants have ________________. They also have ________________.
   They also have ________________.
   ____
   ____

3. Ghosts are ________________. They are ________________.
   They are ________________.
   ____
   ____

4. Aliens from outer space have ________________.
   They also have ________________. They also have ________________.
   ____
   ____

5. Alligators eat ________________. They also eat ________________.
   They also eat ________________.
   ____
   ____

© Great Source. All rights reserved. (5)

Combining Sentences with a Series of Words or Phrases 2

Write Source page 446 explains ways to combine sentences.

Example

Short Sentences: Jon got a baseball on his birthday. He got a T-shirt. He got a parrot.

Combined Sentence: Jon got **a baseball**, **a T-shirt**, and **a parrot** on his birthday.

Combine the following sets of sentences into one sentence. The first sentence has been done for you.

1. Pizza is cheesy. Pizza is gooey. Pizza is great.

   Pizza is cheesy, gooey, and great.

2. Susan is tall. Susan is thin. Susan is left-handed.

3. At camp we play baseball. We jump on trampolines. We go rowing.

4. Marcia goes to the pool. She swims laps. She practices diving.

5. Nina won an art contest. She won a game of miniature golf. She won a 50-yard dash.

© Great Source. All rights reserved. (5)

Directions **Combine the following groups of sentences into one sentence.**

1. Paul mixed some cement. He shoveled it into a wheelbarrow. He pushed it into the garage.

2. Franklin chased the ball. He grabbed the ball. He threw the ball to home plate.

3. Bos has an old dog. He has a new gerbil. He has a blue parakeet. He has a box turtle.

4. Graham read a book about Egypt. He jotted down some notes. He wrote a report about pyramids.

5. The blue jay flew against the window. It fell to the ground. It recovered after a few minutes. It flew away in a flash.

© Great Source. All rights reserved. (5)

Combining Sentences with Phrases

You can combine sentences by moving a phrase from one sentence to another. (See *Write Source* pages 445 and 566.)

Example

Two Sentences: Just then the phone rang. The phone is in the hall.

Combined Sentence: Just then the phone **in the hall** rang.

For each pair of sentences below, underline a phrase from the second sentence that you can move to the first sentence. Then combine the sentences. The first one has been done for you.

1. Something scary happened last night. It happened in our neighborhood.

   Something scary happened last night in our neighborhood.

2. The lights went out. They went out at about 9:00.

   ____

3. Barney started barking like crazy. Barney is our dog.

   ____

4. I was watching TV until the TV went off. I was watching by myself.

   ____

5. I yelled, “Mom!” I yelled with all my might.

   ____

6. She got a flashlight. She took it out of the closet.

   ____

© Great Source. All rights reserved. (5)

Directions **Fill in the blanks to complete the following sentences any way you like. Then combine each pair of sentences. The first one has been done for you.**

1. *Linda* went to the Monroe County Fair. She is my *cousin*.

   Linda, my cousin, went to the Monroe County Fair.

2. ____________ loves chocolate. She is my ____________.

   ____

   ____

3. Mugs is sleeping. He is sleeping ____________.

   ____

   ____

4. I found a box of pennies. I found it ____________.

   ____

   ____

5. ____________ took a trip. He went to ____________.

   ____

   ____

6. ____________ has a horse. It is ____________.

   ____

   ____

© Great Source. All rights reserved. (5)

Combining Sentences with Compound Subjects and Predicates

Another way to combine sentences is to move a subject or verb from one sentence to another. When you do this, you make a **compound subject** or a **compound predicate.** (See *Write Source* page 447.)

Examples

Compound Subject: Carl and Suzanne have pet gerbils.

Compound Verb: Gerbils run through mazes and use exercise wheels.

Combine each set of sentences below by using a compound subject or a compound predicate. The first one has been done for you.

1. Farrah is a gerbil. Festus is a gerbil, too.

   Farrah and Festus are gerbils.

2. Emily takes care of them. Her mom takes care of them, too.

3. Farrah plays in the bathtub! Festus plays in the bathtub, too!

4. Emily and her mom plug the drain. They put in toys.

5. The gerbils can exercise. They can sleep.

© Great Source. All rights reserved. (5)

6. But one day, Emily's mom made a mistake. She left a bath mat over the edge of the tub.

7. Festus grabbed the mat. He climbed out of the tub! He disappeared!

8. Emily and her mom put Farrah in a cage. They went downstairs.

9. Emily searched for Festus. Her mom searched, too.

10. They found Festus in a heat vent. They rescued him.

11. Festus climbed into a tissue box. He was carried to safety.

The Next Step **Now imagine that you are Festus! You are telling Farrah all about your adventure. Write some short, choppy sentences telling what you will say to Farrah. Then trade sentences with a partner and try to combine some of each other's sentences. Use any of the different ways you have practiced so far. We have started Festus's story for you.**

"I was bored. I tried to find Emily. I crawled into a hole. It was dark! . . ."

© Great Source. All rights reserved. (5)

Kinds of Sentences 1

There are four kinds of sentences: **declarative, interrogative, imperative,** and **exclamatory.** (See *Write Source* page 441.)

Examples

Declarative Sentence:
The Sears Tower is a famous skyscraper.

Interrogative Sentence:
How many states can you see from the top of this building?

Imperative Sentence:
You must go to the top.

Exclamatory Sentence:
The people on the ground look like ants!

Recall a time you had an awesome experience. Maybe you went to the top of a skyscraper, got stuck on the top of a Ferris wheel, or rode a dirt bike for the first time. Write one sentence of each kind about your experience.

Declarative: ____

____

Interrogative: ____

____

Imperative: ____

____

Exclamatory: ____

____

© Great Source. All rights reserved. (5)

Kinds of Sentences 2

This activity gives you some practice identifying the four kinds of sentences: **declarative, interrogative, imperative,** and **exclamatory.** (See *Write Source* page 441.)

Write each sentence below into its proper place in the chart.

Where are you?
I'm in the kitchen.
Come here.
Wow, look at the mess!
The kettle of soup boiled over.
Do you need help cleaning the floor?
Yes, get the mop please.
Ouch, the soup is still hot!

Declarative Sentence:

____

____

Interrogative Sentence:

____

____

Imperative Sentence:

____

____

Exclamatory Sentence:

____

____

© Great Source. All rights reserved. (5)

Types of Sentences 1

Read about **simple, compound,** and **complex** sentences on *Write Source* pages 442–444. See model simple sentences, compound sentences, and complex sentences on those pages.

Examples

Simple Sentence: Charlotte is shy.

Compound Sentence: She is quiet, but she can be daring.

Complex Sentence: I like Charlotte because she is like me.

Directions **On the lines below, write *simple, compound,* or *complex* to identify each sentence. The hardest one has been done for you!**

_____________ 1. *The True Confessions of Charlotte Doyle* is a book about a wealthy thirteen-year-old girl named Charlotte.

_____________ 2. In 1832, Charlotte is supposed to sail from England to Rhode Island with two other families, but the families never show up.

_____________ 3. Charlotte decides to sail with the crew alone.

_____________ 4. She remains good friends with the captain, until the captain kills two of the crewmen for being traitors.

_____________ 5. Charlotte then decides to join the crew and becomes "Mr. Doyle" in the logbook.

_____________ 6. During a storm, the first mate is killed with her knife!

complex 7. Avi, the author, wanted to tell his readers that even shy people like Charlotte can become brave.

© Great Source. All rights reserved. (5)

Types of Sentences 2

Review the **types of sentences** on *Write Source* pages 442–444. (You may also read about clauses on page 564.)

Examples

Compound Sentence: I have a 4-H cow, and she is a Black Angus.

Complex Sentence: I named her Midnight because she's as black as night.

Rewrite the following simple sentences. First, add an independent clause (another simple sentence) to make a compound sentence. Then add a dependent clause to make a complex sentence.

1. Raul has new skates.

   Compound: ______________________________

   Complex: ______________________________

   ____

2. Anya's school has a computer club.

   Compound: ______________________________

   Complex: ______________________________

   ____

3. Dad cooks Italian food.

   Compound: ______________________________

   Complex: ______________________________

   ____

© Great Source. All rights reserved. (5)

Simple and Compound Sentences

Recall as much as you can about **simple** and **compound sentences**. Then turn to *Write Source* pages 442–443 and carefully reread the section on simple and compound sentences.

Example

Simple Sentences: My sister wants to earn money for camp.
She will wash cars for $3.00 each.

Compound Sentence: My sister wants to earn money for camp, so she will wash cars for $3.00 each.

Think about a time you did something to earn money. Then write four simple sentences about your experience. Finally, combine the sentences so you have two compound sentences. Check the coordinating conjunctions on *Write Source* page 600, and try to use a different one for each sentence. (See page 443 and 482.3 for more on compound sentences.)

Simple Sentences:

1. ______________________________

2. ______________________________

3. ______________________________

4. ______________________________

Compound Sentences:

1. ______________________________

____

2. ______________________________

____

© Great Source. All rights reserved. (5)

Compound Sentences

See *Write Source* page 443 for help with combining sentences into **compound sentences.**

Example

Simple Sentences: You could go swimming. We could take a walk.

Compound Sentence: You could go swimming, or we could take a walk.

Combine each pair of sentences into one compound sentence. Use a comma and a coordinating conjunction. The first one has been done for you.

1. I made some new friends. They are from other countries.

   I made some new friends, and they are from other countries.

2. Two of them are from Mexico. One is from India.

3. These friends have different holidays. We celebrate all of them.

4. Cinco de Mayo is celebrated in Mexico. Divali is celebrated in India.

5. I don't speak Spanish or Marathi. My friends speak English.

The Next Step **Write a short story about a holiday or custom your family observes. Check to see if any of your short sentences could be combined into compound sentences. Change them.**

© Great Source. All rights reserved. (5)

Complex Sentences 1

One way to combine simple sentences is to make **complex sentences.** You connect two ideas with a **subordinating conjunction.** (See *Write Source* page 444 for an explanation of complex sentences.)

Example

Many French people settled in Canada **while** people from other parts of Europe settled in the United States.

Combine the following pairs of sentences to make complex sentences. Read about subordinating conjunctions on *Write Source* page 600. Choose subordinating conjunctions from the following list: *until, although, since, because, before, when, where.*

1. Millions of Jewish people left Russia. They faced prejudice there.

____

____

2. People from Great Britain found it easy to adjust to the United States. They already spoke English.

____

____

3. Most Irish immigrants came during the 1800s. There was a famine in Ireland.

____

____

© Great Source. All rights reserved. (5)

Directions **Read the paragraph below. Then find and copy the four complex sentences. Finally, circle the subordinating conjunctions.**

When immigrants came to this country in the early 1900s, the first thing many of them saw was the Statue of Liberty. Then they knew that their long sea voyage was over. Before the immigrants were allowed into the United States, they had to talk to government agents. Immigrants then had to stand in another line where a doctor would examine them. They were not sure they could stay, until the agents gave them permission to enter the country.

1. ______________________________

____

____

2. ______________________________

____

____

3. ______________________________

____

____

4. ______________________________

____

____

The Next Step **Now read each sentence above as if it were two sentences. (Take out the subordinating conjunction.)**

© Great Source. All rights reserved. (5)

Complex Sentences 2

One way to combine sentences is to make **complex sentences.** And one way to make complex sentences is with **relative pronouns.** (See *Write Source* page 444 and 580.1.)

Example

Danny, whose brother is in our class, will bring a present.

Use the relative pronoun in parentheses to combine each pair of sentences below. The first one has been done for you.

1. My sister Michelle is having a party. Her birthday is today. *(whose)*

   My sister Michelle, whose birthday is today, is having a party.

2. These cupcakes are for the party. She made them herself. *(which)*

   ____

   ____

3. Her best friend is coming. Her friend lives in Brighton. *(who)*

   ____

   ____

4. I helped put up the decorations. They are in the backyard. *(that)*

   ____

   ____

© Great Source. All rights reserved. (5)

Expanding Sentences with Prepositional Phrases

You can add interesting information and details to your writing by using **prepositional phrases**.

Example

Basic Sentence:
The man was taking a nap.

Expanded with Prepositional Phrases:
The man with the shaggy, brown dog was taking a nap under a tree.
(*With the shaggy, brown dog* and *under a tree* add information and details.)

Directions **In the sentences below, add a prepositional phrase from the list below. The first one has been done for you.**

from their fishing boats	in the city	during the fall migration
of the tropics	with their cheery cheeping	of their apartment buildings

1. The red and black scarlet tanager is a bird *of the tropics*.

2. Common birds ______________________ are English sparrows.

3. Some people like to raise pigeons in cages located on the rooftops ______________________.

4. Parakeets ______________________ entertain elderly people.

5. After flying all day ______________________, geese will often land in grain fields to eat and rest.

6. Seagulls eat what fishers throw back ______________________.

© Great Source. All rights reserved. (5)

Sentence Variety Review 1

Directions **Identify the following sentences as *declarative, interrogative, imperative,* or *exclamatory.***

_______________ 1. Open the umbrella before we get rained on.

_______________ 2. How much rain can fall in one hour?

_______________ 3. The record rainfall of 12 inches in one hour occurred in Hawaii.

_______________ 4. Wow, that was loud thunder!

_______________ 5. Did you see that flash of lightning?

_______________ 6. The storm clouds are full of lightning.

_______________ 7. Let's find some shelter.

_______________ 8. I am really scared!

Directions **Identify the following sentences as "simple," "compound," or "complex."**

_______________ 1. After Jon signed his test, he handed it to the teacher.

_______________ 2. His teacher sent the tests to the central office, and other tests were sent from other classrooms.

_______________ 3. Students' tests were scanned by a super-fast computer.

_______________ 4. When the computer finally stopped, all of the tests had been scored and sorted.

_______________ 5. The tests were returned to the school the following day.

© Great Source. All rights reserved. (5)

Sentence Variety Review 2

In the following review, combine the two short sentences using the conjunction or relative pronoun shown in parentheses. Label the new sentence as *complex* or *compound*. Where there is only one sentence, expand it using one of the prepositional phrases listed below.

in Brighton Park **of the three-story Carnegie Museum**

1. The weather report predicts rain all day. There isn't a cloud in the sky. *(but)*

2. Al wants to be prepared. He is going on a hunger hike. *(who)*

3. Children enjoy the new swing set.

4. The umpire stopped the game. It was raining. *(because)*

5. Nasha went on a picnic. She played volleyball with her friends. *(and)*

6. To find the dinosaur exhibit, Fran's dad looked at a map.

© Great Source. All rights reserved. (5)

Language Activities

Every activity in this section includes a main practice part in which you learn about or review the different parts of speech. Most of the activities also include helpful handbook references. In addition, The Next Step, which is at the end of most activities, encourages follow-up practice of certain skills.

Nouns	**127**
Pronouns	**139**
Verbs	**151**
Adjectives	**163**
Adverbs	**169**
Prepositions	**173**
Conjunctions	**177**
Interjections	**183**
Parts of Speech	**184**

Nouns

A **noun** names a person, a place, a thing, or an idea. (See *Write Source* page 570.)

Examples

Person: mom, Bob, athlete, musician

Place: kitchen, Idaho, park, harbor

Thing: cup, July, truck, highway

Idea: courage, friendship, freedom

Do you ever get your words mixed up? Sam Goldwyn, a famous moviemaker when movies were first invented, used to do that all the time. Below are some of the humorous things that Sam Goldwyn has said. Circle all the words used as nouns. The number after each sentence tells you how many nouns the sentence has. The first sentence has been done for you.

1. "The (scene) is dull; tell him to put more (life) into his (dying)." *(3)*
2. "For your information, I would like to ask a question." *(2)*
3. "It's spreading like wildflowers!" *(1)*
4. "You've got to take the bull by the teeth." *(2)*
5. "This new bomb is dynamite." *(2)*
6. "When I want your opinion, I'll give it to you." *(1)*
7. "This book has too much plot and not enough story." *(3)*
8. "Every director bites the hand that lays the golden egg." *(3)*
9. "I never put on a pair of shoes until I've worn them five years." *(3)*
10. "Look how I developed John Hall: He's a better leading man than Robert Taylor will ever be—someday." *(3; each name counts as 1 noun)*

© Great Source. All rights reserved. (5)

Below are some more "not quite right" things that different people have said. Again, circle all the words used as nouns.

1. "That guy's out to butter his own nest." *(2)*
2. "You are out of your rocker." *(1)*
3. "I'd like to have been an eardropper on the wall." *(2)*
4. "It's time to swallow the bullet." *(2)*
5. "I'm sticking my neck out on a limb." *(2)*
6. "That's a horse of a different feather." *(2)*
7. "You buttered your bread, Now lie in it!" *(1)*

The Next Step **Can you figure out what these people meant to say? Choose three of the sentences above. Then rewrite them so that they are correct. Circle the nouns in your sentences. The first one has been done for you.**

1. *That guy is out to feather his own nest.*
2. ________________
3. ________________
4. ________________
5. ________________
6. ________________
7. ________________

© Great Source. All rights reserved. (5)

Common and Proper Nouns

A **common** noun is any noun that does not name a specific person, place, thing, or idea. Common nouns are not capitalized. A **proper** noun names a specific person, place, thing, or idea. Proper nouns are capitalized. (See *Write Source* page 408 and 570.1–570.2 if you need an explanation of these terms.)

Examples

Common Nouns:	name	book	holiday
Proper Nouns:	Maria	*Write Source*	Memorial Day

Underline each word used as a noun in the sentences below; then write "C" above each common noun and "P" above each proper noun. (Notice that the number of nouns is given in parentheses after each sentence.) The first noun has been marked for you.

P

Juan bought a bike from Green's, a hardware store in the neighborhood. *(5)* He bought a secondhand bike, and it seemed to be in very good condition. *(2)* He bought the bike on Saturday, and rode it around on Sunday, but on Monday the handlebars got very loose. *(5)* On Tuesday, he took his bike back to the store and told Mr. Green, the owner, about the handlebars. *(6)*

Mr. Green got out his wrench and a couple of bolts and fixed the handlebars right away! *(5)* Now Juan thinks his secondhand bike is better than all the new bikes at Green's. *(4)*

© Great Source. All rights reserved. (5)

Directions

Look around you and notice all the persons, places, things, and ideas. Then make two lists—one of proper nouns and one of common nouns. See how many nouns you can spot!

Proper Nouns	Common Nouns

The Next Step Write a sentence that uses one common and one proper noun. Share your sentence with the class.

© Great Source. All rights reserved. (5)

Concrete and Abstract Nouns

Concrete nouns name things that can be touched or seen. **Abstract nouns** name things that cannot be touched or seen. (See *Write Source* 570.3–570.4.)

Examples

Concrete Nouns: flower cake Mr. Taylor

Abstract Nouns: joy party poverty

Sort the nouns below into concrete and abstract nouns. Write each noun in the correct column. Then add one noun of your own to each list.

question	happiness	opinion	thumbs
horse	book	day	liberty
teeth	plot	years	sun
dynamite	egg	nest	trust

Concrete Nouns	Abstract Nouns
____________	____________
____________	____________
____________	____________
____________	____________
____________	____________
____________	____________
____________	____________
____________	____________
____________	____________

© Great Source. All rights reserved. (5)

In the sentences below, underline the nouns and label them "C" for concrete or "A" for abstract. The first one has been done for you.

1. The boy (C) had a question (A) for his teacher (C).
2. All the students listened to the answer.
3. Hitting a baseball well is not easy.
4. Alex says happiness will be getting the cast off his arm.
5. That girl has very good table manners.
6. A loose tooth can cause pain and frustration.
7. The builders will finish the bridge in three months.

The Next Step Write two sentences, each using one concrete noun and one abstract noun. An example has been done for you. (You may—but don't have to—use some of the nouns on the previous page.)

1. *Today in class, we talked about democracy.*
2. ______________________________

____

____

3. ______________________________

____

____

© Great Source. All rights reserved. (5)

Singular and Plural Nouns

A **singular noun** names one person, place, thing, or idea. A **plural noun** names more than one person, place, thing, or idea. (See *Write Source* page 572.)

Examples

Singular Nouns: sister dog car

Plural Nouns: sisters dogs cars

In the following sentences, underline each word used as a noun. (The number of nouns is given in parentheses.) Label each noun "S" for singular and "P" for plural. The first sentence has been done for you.

1. My little brother eats oatmeal for breakfast every weekday morning. *(4)*
2. My mom eats cornflakes and toast or muffins. *(4)*
3. She drinks two cups of coffee, too. *(2)*
4. On weekends we have pancakes, waffles, or scrambled eggs. *(4)*
5. Danny eats his pancakes with butter and jam instead of syrup. *(5)*
6. Our grandparents eat a big breakfast every day. *(3)*
7. They make eggs, bacon, fried potatoes, and cinnamon rolls. *(4)*
8. When Danny goes to visit them, they make oatmeal for him. *(2)*

The Next Step **Write a paragraph about breakfast. Your paragraph could be about what you eat for breakfast, what you would like to eat for breakfast, the weirdest breakfast you can imagine, or any other breakfast subject! When you finish, trade paragraphs with a partner. Underline all the nouns in each other's paragraph. Then label each noun "S" for singular or "P" for plural.**

© Great Source. All rights reserved. (5)

Gender of Nouns

The **gender** of a noun means that something is masculine, feminine, neuter, or indefinite. (See *Write Source* 572.3.)

Examples

Masculine: boy
Feminine: girl
Neuter: closet
Indefinite (male or female): child

In the following sentences, underline and identify the nouns as "F" for feminine, "M" for masculine, "N" for neuter, or "I" for indefinite. The first sentence has been done for you.

1. That boy's (M) favorite clothes (N) are jeans (N) and a sweatshirt (N).
2. Girls sometimes have mirrors in their lockers.
3. Parents want their children to be happy.
4. Gophers dig holes in the ground.
5. The pilot of the plane announced a delay for the afternoon flight.
6. All of the students groaned because they would have to wait two more hours.
7. The class was the last one to arrive at the national science fair.
8. Mr. Acker, our English teacher, has two daughters, one niece, and three sisters.
9. Sometimes the grandson of a king inherits the kingdom.

The Next Step **Write a paragraph about your friends. Exchange papers and underline all the nouns. Then label each noun "M" for male, "F" for female, "N" for neuter, and "I" for indefinite.**

© Great Source. All rights reserved. (5)

Uses of Nouns

Nouns can be used in different ways in sentences. You've had lots of practice using **subject nouns**, which are nouns used as the subject of a sentence. But you also need to know how to use **predicate nouns** and **possessive nouns**. (Read about all three uses on *Write Source* page 574.)

Examples

Subject Noun: My sister went to the library.

Predicate Noun: My sister is an artist.

Possessive Noun: My sister's friends like me.

In the sentences below, label all the underlined nouns. Write an "S" above the noun if it is a subject noun, a "P" if it is a predicate noun, and a "POS" if it is a possessive noun. The first sentence has been done for you.

1. A beagle (S) is a friendly dog (P).
2. The party will be a surprise.
3. Jeremy's cat is a Siamese.
4. Marla's favorite sport is baseball.
5. Jordan became an editor.
6. The winner was Suzanne.
7. Blake knows Lydia's brother.
8. The book's author signed my copy.
9. Our school's track team won the championship.
10. My best hiding place is the attic.

© Great Source. All rights reserved. (5)

Above each underlined noun, write "S" if it is a subject noun, "P" if it is a predicate noun, and "POS" if it is a possessive noun. (Draw an arrow from each predicate noun to the subject it renames.) The first two have been done for you.

The Frog's Tail *(a West African folktale)*

In the beginning, Frog was the only animal that didn't have a tail. The other animals teased him. They said Frog was a freak. So Frog begged Nyame, who had made all the animals, to give him a tail.

Nyame gave Frog a tail. In return, Nyame said Frog must be Nyame's guard. Frog's job was to guard Nyame's magic well. Nyame told Frog that when it didn't rain for a long time, the other wells would dry up. When that happened, Frog should let all the animals come and drink at Nyame's well.

Well, Frog became a bully. Not only did he have a tail, he also had an important job. Soon the rain stopped. All the other wells dried up. The animals came to Nyame's well. But Frog remembered how they had made fun of him, and he wouldn't let them drink.

When Nyame heard what Frog had done, he took Frog's tail away. Ever since then, young frogs have tails, but they lose them as they grow up.

© Great Source. All rights reserved. (5)

Nouns as Objects

A noun is a **direct object** when it receives the action of the verb. A noun is an **indirect object** when it names the person to whom or for whom something is done. A noun is an **object of a preposition** when it is part of a prepositional phrase. (See *Write Source* 574.4 for more information about nouns as objects.)

Examples

Direct Object: Dennis rides his **bike**.

Indirect Object: He gave **Wendy** a ride.

Object of a Preposition: They rode to the **market**.

Look at the following sentences and the circled nouns in each. Then label each noun according to which kind of object it is. The first one has been done for you.

1. Yelena wrote a funny (letter). _direct object_
2. Yelena wrote (Mike) a funny letter. ______
3. Yelena wrote a funny letter to (Mike). ______
4. Mom took (me) to the dentist. ______
5. The teacher wrote on the (chalkboard). ______
6. Mr. Marple asked (Rhonda) to mow the lawn. ______
7. Dr. Fine gave some (medicine) to me. ______
8. Our dog jumped into the swimming (pool). ______
9. Peggy cooked (dinner) for the whole family. ______
10. Ty drew (Carla) a picture. ______

© Great Source. All rights reserved. (5)

Now write three sentences of your own. Each one should contain a noun used as a different kind of object. Your sentences may contain more than one kind of object. *Special Challenge:* You may want to include compound objects in your sentences, just as you sometimes use compound subjects. Check out this example:

(object of a preposition) *(direct object)*

With her new pen, Yelena wrote Mike and Maggie a funny letter.

(compound indirect object)

Note: **Don't underline or label the objects in your sentences.**

1. ______

2. ______

3. ______

The Next Step When you're finished, exchange your work with a classmate. Find and label the nouns used as objects. Did your partner write at least one example of each?

© Great Source. All rights reserved. (5)

Person of a Pronoun

The **person of a pronoun** indicates the point of view of a story. (Read about person of pronouns on *Write Source* page 412 and 576.3–576.5.)

Examples

First-Person Point of View:
I cleaned and scrubbed the cottage all day.

Second-Person Point of View:
You two will go to the ball to meet the prince.

Third-Person Point of View:
She had to leave the ball by midnight.

In the following sentences, underline the personal pronouns. Above each pronoun, write a 1, 2, or 3 to show whether it is a first-person, second-person, or third-person pronoun. The first sentence has been done for you.

1. I (1) heard that the prince invited everyone in the kingdom to the ball. *(1)*
2. My stepmother said, "You stay here and clean. They will go to the ball." *(3)*
3. They left a little later. *(1)*
4. My fairy godmother appeared, and suddenly I became a princess. *(2)*
5. I was thrilled to meet the prince, and he was happy to meet me. *(3)*
6. At midnight, I ran from the ball, leaving the prince wondering who I was. *(2)*
7. He found one of my glass slippers and began searching for the one he loved. *(3)*
8. He finally found me, and we lived happily ever after. *(3)*

The Next Step **Write another ending to *Cinderella* from the first-person or third-person point of view. Share your story endings and decide which point of view was used in each of them.**

© Great Source. All rights reserved. (5)

Number of Pronouns

Review the "Uses of Personal Pronouns" chart on *Write Source* page 578. Notice the pronouns *you, your,* and *yours* can be **singular** or **plural**.

Examples

Singular: I forgot my sandwich. Mary, you can buy your lunch.

Plural: Bill and Mary, when the cooks serve tacos on Friday, they offer a special discount. You can buy two for the price of one.

In the following story, underline the personal pronouns. Above each pronoun, write "S" for singular and "P" for plural.

One day, my friends and I decided to build a sand castle. We had seen amazing pictures from contests, and we thought we could build a simple one. I told my friends that we would need buckets and shovels. They were already at the beach when I arrived. I saw a hot-dog stand run by a man from our neighborhood. He waved at us, and we waved back. We started to dig in the sand and pile it up. My friends began carving towers and walls. Although they had never done this before, their castle looked great. They even put a moat around it, and then they put a drawbridge across the moat. My friends Jill and Serena said, "Would you go buy us some hot dogs and something to drink?" We enjoyed building our castle, and we later saw it wash away in the tide.

© Great Source. All rights reserved. (5)

Subject and Object Pronouns

A **pronoun** is a word used in place of a noun. A **subject pronoun** is used as the subject of a sentence. An **object pronoun** is used after an action verb or a preposition. (See *Write Source* 578.1–578.2.)

Examples

Subject Pronoun: I like movies.

Object Pronoun: Sheila asked if Bob likes them.

Each sentence below contains a subject pronoun, an object pronoun, or both. (Some sentences contain three or four pronouns.) Underline and label each subject pronoun "S" and each object pronoun "O." The first sentence has been done for you.

1. Sheila and I (S) went to a movie.
2. She liked it, but it was too scary for me.
3. After the movie, Sheila's parents, Mr. and Mrs. Daly, took us to a bakery for cupcakes.
4. "You can have any flavor, girls," Mrs. Daly said.
5. "You get a cherry, I will get lemon, and we can share," Sheila said.
6. "Mark is sick," Mrs. Daly said. "We will get a cupcake for him, too."
7. Sheila reminded her that he likes vanilla.
8. "Hey, what about me?" Mr. Daly asked.
9. "No cupcakes for you; you are on a diet!" Mrs. Daly answered.

© Great Source. All rights reserved. (5)

Directions **In each sentence below, cross out the subject. Replace it with the correct subject pronoun: *he*, *she*, *it*, or *they*. The first one has been done for you.**

1. ~~Sheila~~ She liked the movie.

2. The movie was funny.

3. After the movie, Mr. and Mrs. Daly picked up Sheila and Sue.

4. Mrs. Daly bought cupcakes.

5. Sheila got a cupcake for Mark.

6. Mark likes vanilla cupcakes.

7. Mark thanked Sheila.

The Next Step **All of the sentences above, except one, contain a noun or noun phrase that can be replaced with an object pronoun. (Remember, an object pronoun is used after an action verb or a preposition.) Replace each noun or noun phrase with the correct object pronoun (*him*, *her*, *it*, or *them*). The first sentence will look like this:**

1. Sheila liked it.

2. ____________________

3. ____________________

4. ____________________

5. ____________________

6. ____________________

7. ____________________

© Great Source. All rights reserved. (5)

Possessive Pronouns

A **possessive pronoun** shows ownership. These possessive pronouns function as adjectives before nouns: *my, our, his, her, their, its,* and *your.* These possessive pronouns can be used after verbs: *mine, ours, hers, his, theirs,* and *yours.* (See *Write Source* 578.3.)

Examples

She left **her** purse on the bus.

My cat likes to sit on top of the refrigerator.

This book is **mine**, and that one is **hers**.

Underline the possessive pronouns in the following sentences. The first sentence has been done for you.

1. Did your mom take our videos back to the store?
2. When its wheels spin, it whistles.
3. Their cat wriggled out of its collar.
4. I will give my book report right after you give yours.
5. Her house is farther from school than ours.
6. Are these markers yours or his?
7. His cousins like our school better than they like their own.
8. Our team has more players than your team has.
9. Her class has a different lunch hour than my class has.
10. That school is theirs, and it has its own swimming pool.
11. My project will be finished before yours is finished.

© Great Source. All rights reserved. (5)

Cross out each underlined word or phrase below, and replace it with the correct possessive pronoun. The first one has been done for you.

1. Tim is taking ~~Tim's~~ *his* dog for a walk.
2. Our teacher showed us pictures of our teacher's vacation.
3. Mohan and Jon won first prize for Mohan and Jon's science project.
4. Whose poem is longer, Philip's or Marie's?
5. The bird is building the bird's nest.
6. The party will be at my family's house.
7. Is this Taylor's?
8. Taylor thought it was Taylor's.
9. The storm left damaged buildings in the storm's wake.
10. Those skates are my skates.

The Next Step

Write three sentences of your own that correctly use possessive pronouns.

1. ____

____

2. ____

____

3. ____

____

© Great Source. All rights reserved. (5)

Indefinite Pronouns

An **indefinite pronoun** refers to people or places that are not named or known. (See *Write Source* page 413 and 580.5 for lists of indefinite pronouns.)

Example

Something special is planned for the party.

Underline the indefinite pronouns in the following sentences. Some sentences have more than one indefinite pronoun. The first sentence has been done for you.

1. All of the cookies are gone.
2. Most of the ice cream is gone, too.
3. We need a cowboy hat for the play, but nobody has one.
4. Everybody is studying for the test.
5. Mom said, "Either of you can take the trash out."
6. One of us will have to do it.
7. When we start playing volleyball, anything can happen.
8. All of the players do their best.
9. None of my friends are on my team.
10. The chair got wet because somebody left the window open.
11. We jumped when something made a loud noise downstairs.
12. No one wanted to go and see what it was.

© Great Source. All rights reserved. (5)

Relative and Demonstrative Pronouns

Relative pronouns such as *who, whose, whom, which, that, whoever, whomever, whichever, whatever,* and *what* connect one part of a sentence with another word in the same sentence. A **demonstrative pronoun** like *this, that, these,* and *those* points out or identifies a noun without naming it. (See *Write Source* 580.1 and 580.3.)

Examples

Relative Pronoun: Students **who** will help recycle must sign up today.

Demonstrative Pronoun: Put the shelves here. **These** will hold the glass.

In the following sentences, underline the relative and demonstrative pronouns. Identify them by using an "R" or a "D." The first one has been done for you.

R 1. Aluminum cans, which are everywhere, should be recycled.

_____ 2. Recycling has caught on because this saves money.

_____ 3. A lot of electrical power that aluminum plants use is needed to first get the metal from the ore.

_____ 4. An aluminum company employee whose job deals with recycling says that 90 percent less power is used to melt used cans.

_____ 5. Used cans are wanted because those are an important source for aluminum.

_____ 6. Some students who want to earn money and clean up the land pick up as many cans as possible.

_____ 7. Some states that hope to reduce litter will pay five or ten cents for each returned can.

_____ 8. Many states require a deposit on every new can and these have set up recycling centers in every town.

_____ 9. Whoever grabs a garbage bag and picks up cans off the street can earn some extra money.

© Great Source. All rights reserved. (5)

Pronoun-Antecedent Agreement 1

Antecedent is the name for the noun that a pronoun replaces. Each pronoun in your sentences must agree with its antecedent. (See *Write Source* page 173.)

Examples

My **sister** had fun at **her** first clown camp.
(The pronoun *her* and its antecedent *sister* are both singular, and feminine so the pronoun and its antecedent agree.)

Aunt Marietta and **Uncle Bill** join in the clown parade in **their** city.
(The pronoun *their* and its antecedent *Aunt Marietta* and *Uncle Bill* are both plural, so the pronoun and its antecedent agree.)

Circle the pronouns in each of the following sentences. Draw an arrow to each pronoun's antecedent. If a pronoun does not agree with its antecedent, cross the pronoun out and write the correct pronoun above it. The first one has been done for you.

1. Kerry and Sydney first got the idea of clowning from ~~her~~ *their* aunt and uncle.
2. Clown camp included not only local students but also people from many other states, and they lasted all morning every day for one week.
3. Some people returned to camp so they could learn new tricks.
4. The beginning clowns needed to pick their names.
5. Kerry chose *Peppermint* because it is pink and white.
6. Mom made Kerry's costume of pink polka-dotted material, and she sewed a big plastic hoop in the waist.

© Great Source. All rights reserved. (5)

7. The curly pink wig and costume made Kerry look like a real circus clown when she wore it.

8. Putting on makeup took a long time for Kerry, and I got to help her.

9. Mom told Kerry, "Sydney can draw a big red smile to match your red rubber nose."

10. The goofy shoes and floppy neck ruffle looked perfect; it added pizzazz to the outfit!

The Next Step **Write an interesting sentence about something unusual that you have done. Exchange sentences with a partner. Then write a second sentence that uses a pronoun in place of one of the nouns in your partner's original sentence.**

© Great Source. All rights reserved. (5)

Pronoun-Antecedent Agreement 2

An **antecedent** is the noun that a pronoun replaces. Each pronoun in your sentences must agree with its antecedent. (See *Write Source* page 173.)

Examples

Mom said, "I want to see Niagara Falls."
(The pronoun *I* and the word it replaces, *Mom,* are both singular, so they agree.)

Josh and Tim said they wanted to go in the tunnel behind the falls.
(The pronoun *they* and the words it replaces, *Josh* and *Tim,* are both plural, so they agree.)

Write pronouns in the blanks in the following sentences. Be sure each pronoun agrees with its antecedent. Circle the word or words your pronoun replaces. The first one has been done for you.

1. (Mom) and (Dad) said ___they___ would like to stay on the Canadian side of the falls.

2. After Dad checked into the campground, _________ parked the camper.

3. My brothers and I said that _________ wanted to go see the falls.

4. Even before we could see Niagara Falls, we could hear _________.

5. As the wide river spilled over and thundered down, _________ disappeared in clouds of mist.

6. That night, special lighting cast colors on the mist, making _________ glow like rainbows in the night!

© Great Source. All rights reserved. (5)

7. We needed rain gear to go in the tunnel because _________ was very wet.

8. My brothers and I looked funny in the thin yellow raincoats _________ had to wear, but Mom and Dad looked even funnier.

9. As we stood at the lookout behind the wall of water, we were glad to have the raincoats because _________ protected us from the cold mist.

10. Other people were taking boat tours on *The Maid of the Mist* that carried _________ right into the mist at the base of the falls.

The Next Step **Write a paragraph about a special place you have visited. When you finish, circle all the pronouns you have used. See if you can find the antecedent for each one of them. Sometimes an antecedent is in a previous sentence instead of in the same sentence.**

____

____

____

____

____

____

____

____

____

© Great Source. All rights reserved. (5)

Types of Verbs

Review the information about **verbs** on *Write Source* pages 416–417 and 582 before you do this activity.

Examples

Action Verb: Most dogs **chase** cats.

Linking Verb: Our dog **is** a bulldog.

Helping Verb: He **could** chase a big cat.

Read the following sentences and look at the underlined verbs. Decide whether the verbs are action verbs "A," linking verbs "L," or helping verbs "H." Write the correct letter above each. The first one has been done for you.

1. Rolf, our bulldog, loves (A) doggy biscuits.
2. Those biscuits must taste good, because he hides them everywhere.
3. Then he can snack anytime.
4. I have found biscuits in my shoes.
5. Dad has spotted biscuits under his chewed-up gloves.
6. Rolf chews gloves, too . . . and socks.
7. Oh, yes, and Rolf sneaks cookies, but only the fresh-baked kind.
8. Our family has grown fond of Rolf, though.
9. At least he smells sweet.
10. Rolf always spills my bath powder on his way through the bathroom.

© Great Source. All rights reserved. (5)

Linking Verbs

A **linking verb** links the subject of a sentence to a noun or an adjective in the predicate. (See *Write Source* page 417 and 582.2.)

Examples

Lunch **smells** good.
(The verb *smells* links *lunch* to the predicate adjective *good.*)

Our meal **is** soup.
(The verb *is* links *meal* to the predicate noun *soup.*)

In the following sentences, underline the linking verb and circle the predicate noun or predicate adjective. Then draw an arrow from the predicate noun or predicate adjective back to the subject it is linked to. Place an "N" or an "A" over the word to indicate whether it is a predicate noun or a predicate adjective. The first sentence has been done for you.

N

1. The largest ancient elephant was the imperial wooly mammoth.

2. The huge tusks were weapons used against predators.

3. Mammoths were the monsters of long ago.

4. An ancient man seems small next to such a beast.

5. The mammoth's hair feels coarse.

6. After thousands of years, frozen mammoths in Siberia still look powerful.

7. Mammoths were food for ancient people.

8. For thousands of years, mammoths have been extinct.

The Next Step **Write a sentence for each of the following linking verbs: *is, were, look,* and *appear.* Link two of the subjects to predicate adjectives. Link the other two subjects to predicate nouns.**

© Great Source. All rights reserved. (5)

Helping Verbs

A **helping verb** comes before the main verb. It helps to describe an action or to show the time of the action. (See *Write Source* page 417 and 582.3.)

Examples

We could have cut the tree down.

We will move the driveway instead.

In the sentences below, circle each helping verb and underline the verb it helps. (Three sentences have two different clauses with helping verbs.) The first sentence has been done for you.

1. Shaneesha (was) <u>going</u> to the library.
2. She was working on a book report about *Mississippi Bridge.*
3. I asked her if she would take my books back.
4. She said I should go to the library, too.
5. "Diana might come, too," Shaneesha said, "so we could all work on our book reports."
6. "That would work well since I am planning to do mine today."
7. "So, I shall see you there?"
8. "I will ask my mom if it's okay," I answered.
9. Shaneesha said, "If she says you may come, meet us where we were sitting last week."

© Great Source. All rights reserved. (5)

Underline the verb in each sentence below. Then rewrite each sentence two times, adding a different helping verb each time. (See *Write Source* page 582 for a list of helping verbs.) An example has been done for you.

1. Jamie <u>plays</u> the flute.

   Jamie <u>is</u> playing the flute.
   ____

   Jamie <u>will</u> play the flute.
   ____

2. Tomás helps his little brother.

   ____

   ____

3. Kerry and Jim walk to school.

   ____

   ____

4. We write stories.

   ____

   ____

5. Carlos rides the bus to work.

   ____

   ____

© Great Source. All rights reserved. (5)

Simple Verb Tenses

There are three simple tenses. The **present tense** of a verb states an action that is happening now, or that happens regularly. The **past tense** of a verb states an action that happened at a specific time in the past. The **future tense** of a verb states an action that will take place sometime in the future. (See *Write Source* page 418 and 584.1–584.3.)

Examples

Present Tense:
The cricket, mouse, and cat enjoy talking to one another.

Past Tense:
They pranced about the newsstand half the night.

Future Tense:
The three characters will win the hearts of their readers.

The examples above are about the animals in *The Cricket in Times Square* by George Selden. Now it is your turn to write some sentences about imaginary animals that you have read about or seen in a cartoon. Write at least two sentences for each of the tenses.

Present Tense: ____________________

____

____

Past Tense: ____________________

____

____

Future Tense: ____________________

____

____

© Great Source. All rights reserved. (5)

Directions

Write a brief paragraph about the way you think something was like 50 years ago (food, entertainment, cars). Write your paragraph in the past tense. Now write a paragraph about the way you think something will be like in the future (cars, schools, television). Write your paragraph in the future tense. Share your writing with a classmate.

© Great Source. All rights reserved. (5)

Perfect Tenses 1

The **present perfect tense** states an action that began in the past and is still going on. This tense adds *have* or *has* to the past participle form of the main verb. The **past perfect tense** states an action that began and ended in the past. It adds *had* to the past participle. (See *Write Source* page 419 and 584.4–584.5.)

Examples

Present Perfect: That candle **has burned** for the last 30 hours.

Past Perfect: The forest fire **had burned** out three weeks ago.

In the sentences that follow, write the correct form of the verb, either present perfect or past perfect. The first one has been done for you.

has continued
1. The opening act continue for at least 30 minutes. *(present perfect)*

2. The bypass construction take several months to complete. *(past perfect)*

3. Overflowing rivers flood a large part of the county. *(present perfect)*

4. The long journey to the West Coast begin. *(present perfect)*

5. The tree fall more than 60 feet onto the rocks below. *(past perfect)*

6. The run of salmon move quickly upstream. *(present perfect)*

7. By Thursday evening, the men lose the trail. *(past perfect)*

8. With the arrival of the cold north wind, the time came to put on storm windows. *(past perfect)*

9. The flock of geese fly more than 150 miles so far. *(present perfect)*

The Next Step **Write about the seasons of the year. Write one sentence using the present perfect tense and one sentence using the past perfect tense.**

© Great Source. All rights reserved. (5)

Perfect Tenses 2

The **future perfect tense** states an action that will begin in the future and end at a specific time. It adds *will have* to the past participle of the main verb. (See 584.6.)

Example

By next Friday evening, Rayanne **will have finished** her art project.

In the following sentences, underline the verbs. Label each present perfect tense verb "PR," each past perfect tense verb "PP," and each future perfect tense verb "FP." The first one has been done for you.

1. It's Tuesday, and Chantel has started (PR) to hike this trail.
2. She will have hiked more than 50 miles by Thursday afternoon.
3. Chantel and her parents had planned this trip last winter.
4. After her final hike in August, she will have visited five national parks.
5. Chantel's parents have gone with her on each trail.
6. They had bought a weatherproof camera to record their trips.
7. By mid-September, Chantel will have written a report about her adventures.
8. She has begun to arrange all the photos she took along the trails.
9. Chantel had learned about hiking and camping from her parents.
10. By mid-October, she will have presented her report to her class.

The Next Step **In three sentences, use the future perfect tense to write about three goals you plan to accomplish in the coming months.**

© Great Source. All rights reserved. (5)

Active and Passive Verbs

A verb is **active** if the subject is doing the action, but a verb is **passive** if the subject is not doing the action. (See *Write Source* 586.2.)

Examples

Active: The glacier crushed the land beneath it.
(The subject *glacier* did the action.)

Passive: The land was crushed by the glacier.
(The subject *land* is not doing the action.)

In the paragraph below, underline the verbs and label them "A" for active or "P" for passive. The first one has been done for you.

Glaciers have covered much of North America and have melted away several times over thousands of years. Sometimes mountains were cut in half, and V-shaped valleys were turned into U-shaped valleys by these great rivers of ice. Glaciers carried huge boulders hundreds of miles. Today, these large rocks can be seen throughout northern states such as Minnesota and Wisconsin. The Great Lakes were carved out of soft rock, due to the incredible weight of the ice. At the end of each ice age, the glaciers melted and left soil, rocks, and a lot of water behind. Melting glaciers formed ridges of gravel, lakes, and streams. In fact, glaciers changed this continent dramatically.

The Next Step **Write several sentences about weather using both active and passive verbs.**

© Great Source. All rights reserved. (5)

Irregular Verbs 1

Irregular verbs don't play by the rules! When you make them past tense, you can't just add *-ed* as you do with regular verbs. The only way to learn the past tense and past participles of irregular verbs is to memorize each one. And that takes practice.

Examples

Irregular Verbs: shake shook shaken

catch caught caught

Study the chart of irregular verbs on *Write Source* page 588. Then close your book and fill in the missing words in the chart below.

	present tense	past tense	past participle
1.	blow		blown
2.	bring		brought
3.	draw		
4.	eat	ate	
5.	fly		
6.	hide	hid	
7.	know		
8.	lay *(to put in place)*		
9.	lie *(to recline)*	lay	
10.	run		run
11.	wake		woken

© Great Source. All rights reserved. (5)

Irregular Verbs 2

Irregular verbs are not normal! Whenever you change them to past tense or use them with a helping verb, they change in different ways. The only way to know how they change is to learn the different forms of each verb.

Examples

Irregular Verbs: speak spoke spoken

fly flew flown

Fill in the chart below to see how well you know the different forms for seven of the eight common irregular verbs listed. The first one has been done for you.

Present Tense	Past Tense	Past Participle
see	*saw*	*seen*
	wrote	
drive		
		frozen
	burst	
begin		
		blown
	gave	

The Next Step **Now check your work. Turn to the chart on *Write Source* page 588 and look up each word you filled in. List any verbs that you got wrong, and write a sentence using each one.**

© Great Source. All rights reserved. (5)

Irregular-Verbs Review

This activity is a review of some of the **irregular verbs** you have practiced.

Underline the verb in each sentence below. Then rewrite each sentence two times. The first time, change the verb to past tense. The second time, change the verb to past perfect tense and use the correct past participle form for your main verb. The first sentence has been done for you.

1. Mike brings his turtle to school.

   past tense: Mike brought his turtle to school.

   past perfect tense: Mike had brought his turtle to school.

2. Schuyler eats a box of raisins.

   past tense: ______________________________

   past perfect tense: ______________________________

3. We see our teacher's car.

   past tense: ______________________________

   past perfect tense: ______________________________

4. Amber writes a mystery.

   past tense: ______________________________

   past perfect tense: ______________________________

5. Our neighbor gives us tomatoes.

   past tense: ______________________________

   past perfect tense: ______________________________

© Great Source. All rights reserved. (5)

Proper and Common Adjectives

An **adjective** is a word that describes a noun or a pronoun. Adjectives are used in both the subject and predicate part of the sentence. Adjectives can be common and proper. A **proper adjective** is capitalized. (See *Write Source* page 423 and 590.2.)

Examples

The dog has long ears. The German shepherd chewed on a bone.

Directions **Write four adjectives to describe each dog shown below.**

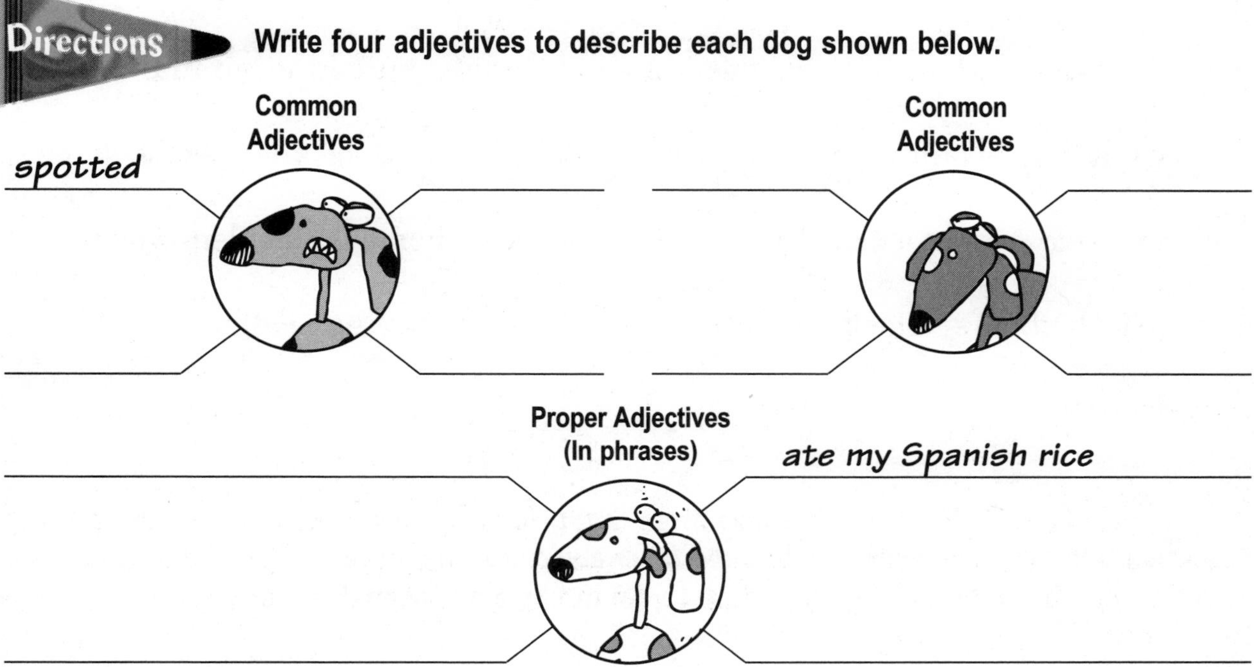

The Next Step **Let's say you have a dog named Ralph. Write a name poem, using common and proper adjectives to describe him. You may use some of the adjectives above, or think of new ones.**

R __________

A __________

L __________

P __________

H __________

© Great Source. All rights reserved. (5)

In the following paragraph, label the adjectives. Write "C" above common adjectives and "P" above proper adjectives. The first one has been done for you. (Note: "Rocky Mountains," "grizzly bears," and "mountain lions" are nouns.)

P

The Colorado Rocky Mountains have a breathtaking appearance that seems almost unreal. The jagged peaks look like the Swiss Alps and cut through gray, hovering clouds. The snow-covered mountainsides reflect blinding sunshine similar to what you would see over the hot Sahara sand of the desert. The massive formations serve as a wilderness home to golden-brown grizzly bears, sleek mountain lions, and towering, long-legged moose.

The Next Step **Below are some adjectives that give only a vague picture of what is being described. After each adjective, write three other adjectives that have similar meanings but are more colorful. Use a thesaurus if you need to. An example has been done for you.**

1. large *gigantic* *tremendous* *extensive*
2. small ______ ______ ______
3. loud ______ ______ ______
4. old ______ ______ ______
5. nice ______ ______ ______
6. fun ______ ______ ______

© Great Source. All rights reserved. (5)

Predicate Adjectives

A **predicate adjective** follows a linking verb and describes the subject. (See *Write Source* 590.3.)

Examples

The fish were luminous in the undersea sunlight.

Our snorkeling adventure became scary when we spotted the barracuda.

In the following paragraph, replace each predicate adjective with a more colorful adjective. The first one has been done for you.

Our family's Florida vacation was ~~fun~~ thrilling. The plane we flew on was big. When I looked out the windows, cars and trucks looked small from thousands of feet up in the air. Buildings and fields were big, like huge patchwork quilts. Roads were long and made odd patterns. Tall, puffy clouds were big, like white mountains right outside our window. Some were fine mist. Others were big, like moving marshmallows. When the sunlight hit a river just right, the light appeared bright, like a camera flash. The speed of the plane became slow, and we spotted the runway and some palm trees. The captain's voice was loud as he announced that we would soon be landing.

© Great Source. All rights reserved. (5)

Indefinite Adjectives

Indefinite adjectives describe approximate amounts of "how much" and "how many." These amounts are estimates rather than exact counts. (See *Write Source* 592.1.)

Examples

There were many people at the car races.

Some rain fell during the day.

Directions **Write a sentence for each of the following words. Use the word as an adjective. The first one has been done for you.**

1. few *Our teacher says few people study the ocean's volcanoes.*
2. many
3. most
4. some
5. all
6. several

© Great Source. All rights reserved. (5)

Forms of Adjectives

Turn to *Write Source* page 424 and read about the **comparative** and **superlative** forms of adjectives. Also read about **irregular forms** at 592.5.

Examples

Positive:	*Comparative:*	*Superlative:*
smart	smarter	smartest
glorious	more glorious	most glorious

In the sentences below, fill in each blank with the correct form of the underlined adjective. The first one has been done for you.

1. Todd's dog is big, but Samantha's dog is ___bigger___, and Charlotte's dog is the ______________ dog I've ever seen.

2. Danielle has many relatives, but Paulo has ______________, and Chet has the ______________ relatives of us all.

3. I'm a bad singer, but my mom is ______________ than I am, and my Uncle Roger is the ______________ singer I know.

4. Katie is funny, but Marsha is even ______________, and Emily is the ______________ of all the girls in our class.

5. Vanilla ice cream is good, but chocolate is ______________, and chocolate chocolate-chip ice cream is the ______________ of all.

6. Summer is a beautiful time of year, but fall is ______________, and spring is the ______________ of all the seasons.

© Great Source. All rights reserved. (5)

Directions **Read the following sentences and then fill in each blank with the correct form of the adjective shown in parentheses. The first one has been done for you.**

1. Shoes come in ___many___ sizes and shapes. *(many)*
2. Though shoes are made from many materials, the __________ ones are made of leather. *(good)*
3. Canvas tennis shoes are __________ than leather tennis shoes. *(cheap)*
4. Synthetic materials make modern hiking shoes __________ than those of the past. *(light)*
5. Even inexpensive hiking shoes are __________ . *(tough)*
6. Steel-toed work boots are __________ than regular boots. *(safe)*
7. After leaving Shoe Mart, Maggie discovered a shoe store at the mall with __________ shoes at reduced prices. *(many)*
8. Men's shoes are often __________ than women's shoes. *(large)*
9. Mom's sandals are her ____________________ footwear. *(comfortable)*
10. Young children think shoes with flashing colored lights are the __________ shoes they could ever have. *(pretty)*
11. Slip-on shoes are __________ for children to put on than tie shoes. *(easy)*
12. Shoes with a steel shank in the sole are __________ than shoes without that support. *(strong)*
13. You can keep your feet __________ in a waterproofed shoe. *(dry)*

© Great Source. All rights reserved. (5)

Types of Adverbs

There are four basic types of **adverbs:** adverbs of *place*, *manner*, *time*, and degree. They describe a verb, an adjective, or another adverb. (See *Write Source* pages 426 and 594.)

Examples

Place: The car swerved left to miss a hole.

Manner: The driver mumbled loudly.

Time: He would complain to the city later.

Degree: For now he was totally relieved.

In each of the following sentences, circle the adverb and draw an arrow to the word it describes. On the line after the sentence, write whether the adverb is one of "place," "manner," "time," or "degree." The first sentence has been done for you.

1. Jody and I often go to the park. *time*
2. Sometimes we play softball. ________
3. We choose our teams carefully. ________
4. We play hard. ________
5. Jody and I always pitch. ________
6. Tasha barely caught the pop fly. ________
7. Ira hits the ball hard. ________
8. Most fielders step back for Ira. ________
9. Monica easily catches ground balls. ________
10. Tyrone completely missed first base. ________

© Great Source. All rights reserved. (5)

Directions **In each of the following sentences, add an adverb of the type in parentheses. Write the new sentence on the line. Then circle the adverb and draw a line to the word it describes. The first one has been done for you.**

1. I'm going to the park. *(time)* I'm going to the park later.
2. Marcia eats. *(manner)* ______
3. Rodrigo laughs. *(manner)* ______
4. Let's go swimming. *(time)* ______
5. Let's go for a walk. *(place)* ______
6. Arlene noticed a robin. *(degree)* ______

The Next Step **Write a personal narrative paragraph about your favorite game, sport, or pastime. Use adverbs to tell about time, place, manner, and degree. Underline all of your adverbs.**

© Great Source. All rights reserved. (5)

Forms of Adverbs

Review *Write Source* pages 426 and 596. Then complete this activity using the different forms of **adverbs**.

Examples

Positive:	*Comparative:*	*Superlative:*
quick	quicker	quickest
softly	more softly	most softly

Rewrite each sentence below. In the first sentence, use the comparative form of the underlined adverb. In the second sentence, use the superlative form of the same adverb. An example has been done for you.

1. Gabriella runs fast.

   Gabriella runs faster than Sarah.

   Teri runs fastest of all.

2. Bruce played well.

3. Larissa plays her CD's loudly.

4. Terrence reads slowly.

© Great Source. All rights reserved. (5)

Directions **Think of three adverbs that describe how something is done. Then write sentences using the positive, comparative, and superlative forms of each adverb. One has been done for you.**

1. adverb = *carefully*

   Jim writes his stories carefully.

   Rosa writes hers more carefully than Jim writes his.

   Clare writes hers the most carefully of all.

2. adverb = ______________________

3. adverb = ______________________

4. adverb = ______________________

© Great Source. All rights reserved. (5)

Prepositional Phrases 1

Turn to *Write Source* pages 429 and 598 and review the information about **prepositions** and **prepositional phrases**.

Example

(preposition)

We have an aquarium 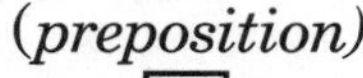.

(prepositional phrase)

In the sentences below, circle each preposition and underline each prepositional phrase. The first sentence has been done for you.

1. Patches ran around the room and then jumped onto the table.
2. Tom is in his room, hiding under his bed.
3. We went to a restaurant before the play.
4. This book was written by my favorite author.
5. After lunch, we have free time until 1:00.
6. My paper is under that pile of books on the desk.
7. Becky left her skates outside the door and went into the house.
8. She walked through the kitchen toward the stairs.
9. My house is near the corner of Fifth Street and Central Avenue.
10. Go past two stop signs and turn right at Fifth Street.

© Great Source. All rights reserved. (5)

Replace the underlined preposition so the new prepositional phrase means the opposite. The first one has been done for you.

1. Frank is walking to the barn. *from*
2. Marie is sitting inside the car.
3. Blaine hit the ball under the fence.
4. After checking the map for the third time, Bill walked down the steps.
5. Elaine spotted a deer in front of the tree.
6. Rafe's little brother jumped on the green couch.
7. After the game, we ate brats, potato chips, and ice cream.
8. Hanna went to the craft fair without her friends.
9. Lane got his lunch and sat down at the table across from Jake.
10. Janelle walked through the deep mud puddle.
11. Ready for the next task, Gere walked out of the gym.

The Next Step **Write three sentences about a weekend activity and use prepositional phrases in the sentences. Then have a partner change each of the prepositions to mean the opposite.**

© Great Source. All rights reserved. (5)

Prepositional Phrases 2

Turn to *Write Source* pages 429 and 598 for more information about **prepositions** and **prepositional phrases**.

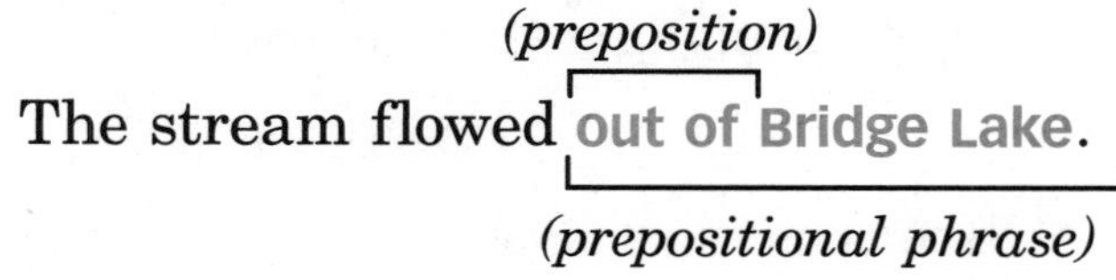

In the sentences below, write an appropriate preposition in each blank provided and then underline the prepositional phrase. The first one has been done for you.

Each summer, my brother Steven and I looked forward to floating ____down____ the stream ____________ our grandfather's cabin. We each slipped big black inner tubes ____________ our heads and jumped ____________ the dock. First, we ducked down as we went ____________ the wooden bridge. Then we stayed close together as we paddled ____________ the cattails and weeds ____________ the meandering stream. I liked to have my brother ____________ the lead. Once he shouted when he saw a water snake swimming ____________ us. Usually, ____________ the clear water, we watched the schools

© Great Source. All rights reserved. (5)

________ minnows swimming ________ us. ________ many bends and some shallow spots, we finally came ________ our favorite spot—a big culvert going ________ a road. Our yells echoed as we shot through ________ the other side. Then we swirled ________ a churning circle ________ a big, gentle whirlpool.

The Next Step **Write a sentence for each of the prepositional phrases below. Illustrate your favorite sentence.**

1. in the house

____

____

2. behind the house

____

____

3. throughout the house

____

____

4. for the house

____

____

© Great Source. All rights reserved. (5)

Coordinating Conjunctions

Coordinating conjunctions connect equal parts. For example, coordinating conjunctions can connect two words, two phrases, or two clauses. (See *Write Source* pages 429 and 600.)

Example

My cookie jar is full, **but** it is full of dog biscuits.

Use one of the following coordinating conjunctions to fill in the blank in each sentence below.

and	but	or	so	yet

1. My dog Harold is small ____________________ strong.
2. He has white paws ____________________ shaggy ears.
3. All afternoon he sleeps on the porch ____________________ in the house.
4. When I get home, he wants to run ____________________ play.
5. Harold is fat ____________________ fast.
6. He chases squirrels ____________________ our cat.
7. Harold is seven years old ____________________ still plays like a puppy.
8. He growls at other dogs ____________________ hides during storms.
9. Harold likes to swim in the lake, ____________________ he doesn't like being out in the rain.

© Great Source. All rights reserved. (5)

Use a comma plus a coordinating conjunction from the list on page 177 to connect each pair of simple sentences below.

1. Harold loves dog food. He loves people food, too.

2. I give Harold cookies. He's always happy to see me.

3. He likes hamburgers. He's not supposed to have them.

4. Harold loves bones. He looks for them in grocery bags.

5. Harold likes to swim in the lake. He chases the Canada geese.

6. Harold barks at our cat. He never barks at strangers.

© Great Source. All rights reserved. (5)

Subordinating Conjunctions

Use a **subordinating conjunction** to connect two clauses to make a complex sentence. (See *Write Source* pages 429 and 600.2.)

Example

We didn't have time to go fishing **although** we had poles and bait.

Choose subordinating conjunctions from the following list and write them on the lines to complete the story.

> after, although, as, because, before, if, in order that, since, so, that, though, unless, until, when, where, while

We were in art class ____________________ our principal reminded us that the dress rehearsal for the concert would begin at 6:00 p.m. sharp! ____________________ Matt missed the rehearsal and arrived just before the concert, the choir director told Matt ________________ he would have to miss out on the party. ____________________ the concert was over, Matt disappeared. We spotted him using the office phone. Later, we were surprised to see that Matt was allowed to be at the party __________________ we heard his reason for being late. His new brother had just been born! __________________ Matt knew he had a new brother, he wasn't sure what the baby had been named.

© Great Source. All rights reserved. (5)

In the exercise below, combine each pair of clauses to form a complex sentence using the subordinating conjunction shown in parentheses. Remember to use correct punctuation and capitalization. The first one has been done for you.

1. the day was sunny   the air was very cold   *(although)*

   Although the day was sunny, the air was very cold.

2. the food was cooked   everyone was served   *(after)*

   ____

3. everyone was surprised   Bob ran into the room   *(when)*

   ____

4. Jamie held the form   Lana filled it with plaster   *(while)*

   ____

5. a part was missing   James couldn't finish the model   *(because)*

   ____

6. Laz didn't have enough trouble   his bike pedal broke   *(as if)*

   ____

7. the bell rang   students could not leave the building   *(until)*

   ____

8. Penny bought the hat   the sale ended   *(before)*

   ____

The Next Step **Using *after, when, though,* and *because,* write several complex sentences about a game you have played with friends.**

© Great Source. All rights reserved. (5)

Conjunctions Review

This activity is a review of coordinating and subordinating **conjunctions**. (See *Write Source* pages 429 and 600.1–600.2.)

Each of the sentences below has one coordinating conjunction and one subordinating conjunction. Underline both, and write "C" above each coordinating conjunction and "S" above each subordinating conjunction. The first sentence has been done for you.

1. Let's shoot baskets or (C) play catch until (S) it gets dark.
2. While it is snowing, we can make a snowman and a snow fort.
3. The new boy doesn't know us, but he'll come to our party if we invite him.
4. My mom and I like to watch videos when it's rainy.
5. When our teacher is sick, Mr. Diaz or another substitute comes to our class.
6. Tina does her homework and her chores before she eats dinner.
7. We heard the kitten mewing, yet we couldn't tell if the sound was coming from the closet.
8. Juan and I walked home after we watched the fireworks.
9. Terri wants to come over, but she can't come unless she gets over her cold.
10. Because it is snowing, school may be canceled or delayed.

© Great Source. All rights reserved. (5)

Add the needed conjunctions to the sentences below. Then write three sentences of your own, using conjunctions and underlining them.

1. ________ our parents aren't home, Jan ________ I are making dinner.

2. Jared ________ my sister walks the dog ________ we leave for school.

3. It's Monday, ________ there is no school ________ it's a holiday.

4. ________ the thunderstorm, the sun came out, ________ the air was still cold, ________ it was windy.

5. ____

____

____

6. ____

____

____

7. ____

____

____

© Great Source. All rights reserved. (5)

Interjections

An **interjection** is a word or phrase used to express a strong emotion or surprise. A comma or an exclamation point is used to separate an interjection from the rest of the sentence. (See *Write Source* page 602.)

Examples

Holy cow! That ball is out of here!

Oh, there it is.

Pretend you have just spent some time with a herpetologist (someone who works with snakes and other reptiles). Write a postcard telling a friend how you felt about being around snakes. Use interjections to let your friend know how strongly you felt about the experience.

_______________, 200 ___

Dear _______________,

USA ¢

From,

© Great Source. All rights reserved. (5)

Parts of Speech Review 1

Directions **Write the part of speech for each list of words on the line in the circle. See *Write Source* page 602 for a list of the eight parts of speech.**

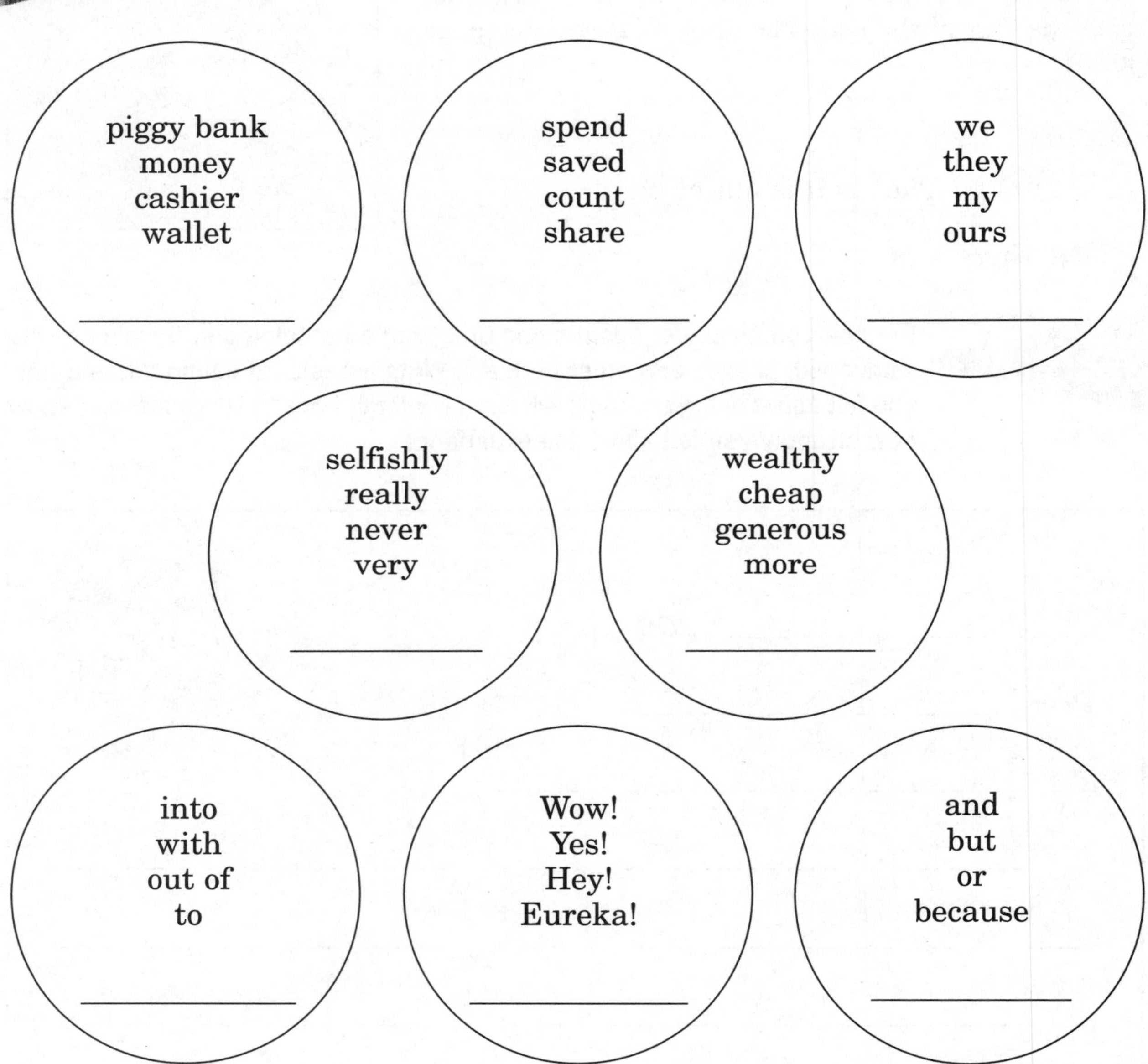

The Next Step **Now write a sentence using as many of the parts of speech as you can. Use some of the words in the circles.**

© Great Source. All rights reserved. (5)

Parts of Speech Review 2

This activity is a review of all the **parts of speech** you have studied.

Below is a fable from Aesop. Above each underlined word, write what part of speech the word is. The first two have been done for you.

The Crow and the Pitcher

noun verb

Once there was a crow who was so thirsty he couldn't speak. He found a large pitcher of water in a garden. He lowered his beak into the pitcher to drink. But there was only a little water in the pitcher, and he couldn't reach it. He thought of breaking the pitcher, but it was too strong. He tried hard to turn the pitcher over, but it was too heavy. The poor crow was about to give up when he noticed some pebbles in the garden. This gave him a wonderful idea. "Yes!" he thought to himself. "I will have a drink after all!" He quickly picked up a pebble in his beak and dropped it into the pitcher. As he did this again and again, the water rose higher and higher in the pitcher. Finally, the crow was able to reach the water and drink.

© Great Source. All rights reserved. (5)

Parts of Speech Review 3

Read the following paragraph. Then fill in the blanks with examples of nouns, verbs, pronouns, and so on, from the paragraph.

I spotted an old picture of a suburb of Milwaukee, Wisconsin. In black and white, this 100-year-old picture showed very tall trees instead of the huge electrical towers that are there today. The trees appeared to be pine trees, but maybe they were cedars. A dirt path that was only about three feet wide stood in place of busy four-lane roads. Wow! For me, it's rather sad to see a quiet rural area grow slowly into a small city.

Nouns	Verbs	Pronouns
______________	______________	______________
______________	______________	______________
______________	______________	______________
______________	______________	______________

Adverbs	Adjectives	Prepositions
______________	______________	______________
______________	______________	______________
______________	______________	______________
______________	______________	______________

Interjections	Conjunctions
______________	______________
	______________

© Great Source. All rights reserved. (5)